Language to go

PRE-INTERMEDIATE

TEACHER'S RESOURCE BOOK

Robin Wileman

with Nanna Challis, Drew Hyde and Kenna Bourke

Series Editor: Simon Greenall

Longman

www.longman.com

Contents

4

The past

Verb patterns

The present

Noun phrases

Modals

The future

Adjectives

Present perfect

Functions

Conditionals

Introduction

About *Language to go*

Many adult students of English have a limited amount of time for their studies. They may require English for both professional and social reasons, and are also aware that they're likely to use it in a number of international situations. They need to ensure that the time they spend on their English learning is highly focused and goal oriented. They need to be able to achieve certain tasks and to leave a language class, sometimes after a busy and tiring day of working or studying, with a bite-sized chunk of *Language to go* and a sense of 'Yes, I can do that – anywhere in the world, in English!'

Language to go is a short course for this kind of adult student. Our underlying principle is that students start the class with an objective defined in terms of a realistic outcome, and finish with the language they need to achieve it. So here's a quick overview of what the course contains:

- Four levels: Elementary, Pre-Intermediate, Intermediate and Upper Intermediate. Each level has 40 teaching lessons, and each lesson has been carefully written so that it takes around 60 minutes in the classroom.
- A Practice section, a Grammar reference and the recording scripts at the back of the Students' Book.
- A detachable Phrasebook in the Students' Book.
- A class cassette or CD with the listening material.
- This Teacher's Resource Book, containing a step-by-step guide to every lesson (including answer keys), photocopiable activities, photocopiable tests and a Writing bank.
- The *Language to go* website (www.language-to-go.com).

Language to go – a closer look

Students' Book

Content

Each teaching lesson is designed to last 60 minutes and is contained on two facing pages, which reinforces visually the relationship between the Students' Book lesson and the classroom lesson. It focuses on a final activity, by presenting and practising the language required and then inviting students to perform the activity at the end of the lesson. The lesson begins with a presentation of the vocabulary needed for the final activity, then continues with reading or listening material which presents the target structure(s) in a meaningful context. This is followed by some inductive grammar work, focusing on the meaning and the form of the structure, and by some practice exercises. Students should now be equipped to do the final activity in the *Get talking* section at the end of the lesson, which is sometimes accompanied by a *Get writing* section. The *Language to go* is exemplified in an easily memorised dialogue in the bottom corner of each right-hand page and acts as the focus and goal of the lesson.

Motivation is at the core of successful learning in general, and language learning in particular; we have therefore taken great care to choose topics and texts which will stimulate the student intellectually as well as linguistically. Much of the material has been chosen so that it reflects the international community of English users, as native or non-native speakers.

We have tried to use as many international contexts as possible, since we're aware that our students will use their newly acquired linguistic competence not just in their own country or in an English-speaking one, but all around the world.

Cyclical syllabus

The course design of Pre-Intermediate, Intermediate and Upper Intermediate is based on a **cyclical syllabus**, in which different aspects of language, such as tenses, modals, vocabulary or functions, are presented several times in the same level. The advantage of this approach is that the structures can be naturally revised, recycled and consolidated on a regular and frequent basis. It also allows schools and institutes with a system of continuous enrolment to ensure that students who arrive later in the course are not disadvantaged by missing out on lessons which have already dealt with key structures.

At Elementary level, we have not used a cyclical syllabus, as it does not meet the needs of Elementary students, for whom a specific sequence of acquiring language is more useful. It is also true that this level lends itself less well to courses with continuous enrolment.

The principal **syllabuses** in the course are Grammar and Vocabulary. The approach to grammar is largely one of guided discovery in which the students are presented with examples of the target structure and then invited to work out the rules relating to form and meaning. Much of the vocabulary is presented in chunks as well as individual words, to reflect the way we use English in real life.

Skills

The **skills** of reading, listening, writing and speaking are all practised. Speaking is at the core of the philosophy of *Language to go*, and is the skill most often practised, both in the *Get talking* sections and in the pair and group work activities. The reading and listening material includes examples of English which may be beyond the immediate level of students, but is treated in a way which prepares them for dealing with it in a real-life context. Writing is deliberately not practised extensively, since we feel that it is a skill which can be more usefully developed outside the classroom, allowing the interactive opportunities of the classroom to be exploited to their maximum on a short course. However, several lessons also include a *Get writing* activity, and further guidance is given in the Writing bank in this book.

Pronunciation is dealt with wherever it is appropriate to the grammar or the vocabulary syllabus strands, focusing on stress in words, stress in sentences and intonation patterns rather than individual phonemes.

Additional material

The **Practice section** provides further exercises to consolidate the language taught in the main lesson. For teachers who have classes lasting longer than 60 minutes, it can be used in class, either after the *Practice* exercises or at the end of the main lesson. The exercises in the Practice section can also be set for homework and have been written so that students can work on them alone.

The **Grammar reference** is designed to be a more descriptive explanation of the grammar points covered in the main teaching lesson.

Phrasebook

This is a reformulation of some of the language taught in the course, as well as a reminder of other relevant words and expressions which are appropriate to the level, and presented in a familiar phrasebook style. A traditional phrasebook, with its list of useful words and expressions, is at the core of the concept of *Language to go*; in other words, language which is organised and can be readily accessed when required in real-life situations.

Teacher's Resource Book

This book contains:
- a lesson-by-lesson contents map;
- this introduction, with an overview of the course;
- some tips on how to make the most of the material;
- a personal statement from the authors;
- how *Language to go* links with external examinations;

- a phonemic chart;
- step-by-step Teaching notes for each lesson including answer keys;
- photocopiable activities;
- photocopiable Tests with answer key;
- photocopiable Writing bank.

Photocopiable activities

Teachers who have more than 60 minutes' class time available may wish to provide further skills practice, so we have provided some extra material. There are 40 extra activities, each one corresponding to a Students' Book lesson, which are designed to be photocopied and distributed to the students. Each activity will provide a further twenty to 30 minutes' practice of the language taught in the lesson. The teaching notes opposite each photocopiable activity are for your reference, providing a guide to how the activity should be organised and answer keys where relevant.

Photocopiable tests and answer keys

These are to be used to check on the students' progress at regular intervals during the course. There are four for each level, and they focus on the vocabulary and grammar covered in every ten lessons. So the ideal time to do these tests will be when you have finished Lessons 10, 20, 30 and 40.

Photocopiable writing bank

This can be used at any point in the course when you think it appropriate for students' needs, or to help guide them with a particular *Get writing* activity.

The *Language to go* website

By clicking onto www.language-to-go.com, you will find material of interest to both students and teachers, including further interactive practice exercises for each lesson. There are also self-study versions of the main Grammar / Language focus of each lesson, and these serve as useful review exercises.

Language to go is an exciting and innovative course of international English. It combines the basic requirements of a tightly focused and minimalist short course with the wealth of materials appropriate to the learning potential of adults in the 21st century. It contains topics and texts designed to motivate adult students with social and professional reasons for learning English. It has been written with a mixture of enthusiasm, passion and pedagogical rigour by a team of talented authors, and produced by editors, designers, researchers and many others with much love and care. So, now it's over to you with *Language to go*. We hope you and your students enjoy it.

Simon Greenall
Series Editor

A few ideas for classroom procedures

Personalisation

Most adult students of English are willing to trust their teachers because they believe everything they do is in their best interests. But now and then, they must ask themselves, 'Why am I doing this? How is this relevant to me?' When this happens, both student and teacher are faced with a potential challenge to their motivation.

Personalisation allows students to relate material to their own world. It is therefore a key factor in maintaining their motivation, especially during challenging activities like roleplays. The teacher has to make sure the student understands how an activity relates to their language-learning needs. Every activity in *Language to go* is designed to allow maximum personalisation for students. The lessons are all constructed around a final activity, and these activities will usually provide an opportunity for them to adapt the language being used to their own circumstances. For example, during the presentation of a new topic, there is usually an appeal to the student to think about how much they might know about it. On other occasions, there may be an invitation to use the target vocabulary or grammar in sentences which are relevant to the student.

If you feel that personalisation might be lacking at any stage, for example, after a vocabulary exercise, you could suggest that students choose four or five words which they think might be useful to them, or which look like words in their language, or which sound nice, or which they can place in categories of their own choice. After a grammar activity, encourage students to write a couple of sentences about themselves using the target structure. You don't need to correct these extra activities, although you may want to ask them to share their answers with the rest of the class. In this way, personalisation can have two purposes: to consolidate the learning process and to make what they're doing relevant to themselves.

Vocabulary

The words and expressions which form the focus of the Vocabulary sections are those which we think are important at this level. Most lessons only contain between eight and ten items for productive learning (that is, words which the student should be able to use in spoken or written work, and not words which they are able to recognise).

Many of the vocabulary items are grouped in topics; others are grouped according to some of the rules behind word formation or collocation in English.

Encourage students to keep a vocabulary list containing all the items which they have learnt. Try to ensure that the list categorises the words in different ways, in order to consolidate the learning process.

When students ask for help in understanding words, try not to explain too many immediately, but ask them to help each other, or to use dictionaries if they're available in the classroom. Remember also that explaining new words may build their vocabulary, but it may not develop their ability to work out the meaning of words in reading and listening activities.

Speaking

There are many opportunities for speaking practice in *Language to go*. Firstly, there are many pair and group work activities based on a reading, listening, grammar or vocabulary task. Secondly, there are some lessons which focus on functional language where there is a clear model of the language to be used. Thirdly, most of the final activities in the lesson (*Get talking*) are opportunities to practise speaking. Remember to aim for a balance between accuracy and fluency; not every activity needs your close and careful correction of errors.

Listening

The listening material contains examples of everyday, natural spoken English. Students may be worried by the speed of delivery, thinking that it's too fast, so reassure them that this is also quite normal in real life, and that the classroom is the best place to be exposed to this type of natural language. They don't need to speak as fast themselves, but they do need practice in understanding authentic spoken English. The following guidelines should help them:

- Encourage students to focus on the main ideas of the listening passage and not get distracted by words they don't understand. The main activity will usually help them to do this.

- Help them to interpret clues from the context (situation, tone of voice etc.). This will usually enable them to understand a great deal more than the words will convey.

- Play the recording a couple of times (more than this will start to compromise their motivation), even if the instructions only suggest once.

- Try not to play the recording and stop after every phrase, as this will not give them the important practice in listening to the discourse of spoken English.

Writing

Writing is usually suggested in the *Get writing* sections as a way of showing that students have mastered the language which has been focused on in the lesson. They are all meant to be classroom versions of situations they may encounter outside the classroom – letters, e-mails, exam-style essays etc. The *Writing bank* in this Teacher's Resource Book provides photocopiable models of these writing genres with accompanying suggestions on how to exploit them in class.

Encourage students to practise a form of *process writing*: ask them to write down as much as they can without worrying too much about being accurate. Then ask them to reread what they have written, or maybe even show it to a partner. Encourage them to be critical and to revise their work if necessary. Then ask them to write a final version which incorporates extra ideas and all their corrections. Remember that writing can be an exercise in fluency as well as accuracy.

Reading

Much of the reading material involves words which students may not have come across, just like in real life. Many of the accompanying activities are designed both to support their general understanding of the passage as they read it, and to check their comprehension afterwards.

Try not to answer questions about difficult words, but instead, encourage students to work out the meaning for themselves.

Make sure that students read the passage once, perhaps at the end of the lesson, just to enjoy it, to respond with natural interest to it and without having to answer difficult questions!

Roleplays

The roleplays are presented as a further opportunity for students to practise speaking. Some students enjoy roleplays, especially in a foreign language. Others find they make enormous demands on their imagination. For this reason, we have tried to provide suitable support into the roleplays, so that less imaginative or creative students don't feel under pressure to come up with all the ideas themselves. Go round the pairs or groups as they are doing the roleplays, listening but not interrupting, unless they want help in what they need to do.

Try to avoid correcting students as they are doing their roleplays, but make a note of major mistakes, if you wish, and discuss them with the whole class at the end of the lesson.

Error correction

It's a good idea to think about what and when you correct before the lesson begins. Make this decision part of your lesson plan.

It's best to avoid correction during an activity which focuses on fluency until after it's over; on the other hand, it may be best to correct students in an activity which focuses on accuracy as they do it. Look at each activity in turn, decide what its aim is and choose the best strategy.

Remember that less-confident students will need more encouragement than others, and your correction may compromise their motivation.

You may also decide you only want to indicate the student has made an error rather than correct it yourself. Think carefully about your attitude to error correction, and share your opinions with the whole class.

Jigsaw reading

Some activities involve a technique known as *jigsaw reading*. This involves students working in pairs. The first instruction will be to work separately on a reading passage, with separate but complementary tasks to perform. This usually involves them turning to a specified text or activity in the *Information for pair and group work* section at the back of the Students' Book. The second instruction will be to work together and to share the information they have gathered from the separate tasks.

This technique is at the very heart of communicative language teaching, as it involves an information gap (Student A knows something that Student B doesn't, and vice versa) and a meaningful exchange of information during the second stage of the activity, where the students tell each other what they have learnt.

As long as the students understand the instructions, it's best for the teacher simply to signal the start of the two stages of the activity, and listen as the pairs/groups perform it. You can finish the activity sequence with group feedback to check the answers are correct.

Pronunciation

Pronunciation work in *Language to go* focuses more on word and sentence stress and intonation patterns than on individual phonemes. There are several techniques you can use:

* *Drilling* can be individual or choral repetition of a word or a sentence. Choral repetition with the whole class is a way of building up students' confidence in pronouncing strange words or new sentences.

* *Backchaining* involves the repetition of different parts of a sentence, often starting at the end, and gradually adding parts until you have reconstituted the whole sentence.

* *Word linking* focuses on the fact that when you say words in connected speech, the individual phonemes which make up the word may change. Say the words separately, then say them in connected speech and emphasise the way in which they sound different.

The *Language to go* authors

Gillie Cunningham
and Sue Mohamed

Gillie Cunningham and Sue Mohamed

We met in 1980 at International House English Language School, London. Sue had just returned from seven years' teaching English as a Foreign Language in Libya. She had also taught English for a year in the Lebanon and French for two years in state schools in London. Gillie had been living in Canada, where she worked in a school for students with learning disabilities. She had also taught English as a Foreign Language in Greece. We became close friends. Sue soon got itchy feet and wanted to travel again. She left England with her eight-year-old daughter, Emma, and worked as a teacher/teacher-trainer in Egypt. After a short time back in England, they went to France, where Sue worked as an English Teaching Adviser at the British Council in Paris. She then returned to England and became Head of Teacher Training at International House, London. She also began writing ELT books.

Gillie was now teaching/teacher-training at the Bell Language Schools in Cambridge and Saffron Walden. In 1992, she became Joint Chief Assessor of the RSA/UCLES Diploma for Teachers of English as a Foreign Language to Adults (DTEFLA). During this time, Gillie had also had a daughter called Amybeth. This did not stop Gillie travelling to work in a variety of countries, including Italy, Spain, Ecuador and Argentina, where she gave training seminars and presentations at ELT conferences. She also began writing ELT books.

When we met up again, fifteen years after working in London together, we resumed our close friendship. Apart from our children, our other loves are reading, the cinema, art, the theatre and music. On occasion, you might even find us in a local gym! We continue to work with foreign students and teachers from many different countries. Gillie is currently Assistant Academic Manager at the Bell School, Saffron Walden. Sue is now a full-time writer and has recently worked as a consultant on textbook writing projects in Romania and Mongolia. In 1998, we began writing ELT books together.

In our years of teaching/teacher-training and writing, we have become increasingly aware of the demand from teachers and students for a short, grammatically and lexically based coursebook. Adult students with limited time available for studying say they want to maximise the use of language learnt in the classroom. They want a course which will help them understand the systems of English at whichever point they join that course. For these reasons, we were excited at the prospect of working on *Language to go*.

Here was a short course which would allow students to appreciate that a single exposure to a particular language form did not mean it had been learnt. By using a cyclical syllabus, students could systematically revise a grammatical form and extend their understanding of its uses. By having a principled approach to the teaching of lexical fields and lexical systems, students would systematically increase their vocabulary. At the end of each lesson, the *Language to go* box would illustrate the learning objectives in a short, easily remembered dialogue.

The initial excitement and enthusiasm we had continued throughout this writing project. We hope students and teachers will benefit from and enjoy using the book as much as we have enjoyed writing it.

Gillie and Sue

Language to go and EFL exams

The table below shows *general* equivalences between the four levels of *Language to go* and two well-known international examination boards, UCLES (University of Cambridge Local Examinations Syndicate) and Trinity College, in terms of the language taught and the topics covered in the four books.

While *Language to go* is not an examination preparation course, a student who has, for example, completed the Elementary level would have sufficient language to attempt UCLES KET, and start a preparation course for UCLES PET. Examination training is required for all EFL examinations, and we would strongly advise students to follow an examination preparation course. But you will find that some of the exercises in the Students' Book lessons, the Practice section and the photocopiable Tests are similar in format to those found in EFL public examinations.

Note that higher-level exams, such as UCLES CPE and ESOL Grades 11–12, are not covered in this table.

For further information, contact:

UCLES
English as a Foreign Language
1 Hills Road
Cambridge
CB1 2EU
United Kingdom
Tel: +44 (0) 1223 553355
Fax: +44 (0) 1223 460278
E-mail: eflhelpdesk@ucles.org.uk
www.ucles.org.uk

Trinity College
89 Albert Embankment
London
SE1 7TP
United Kingdom
Tel: +44 (0)20 7820 6100
Fax: +44 (0)20 7820 6161
E-mail: info@trinitycollege.co.uk
www.trinitycollege.co.uk

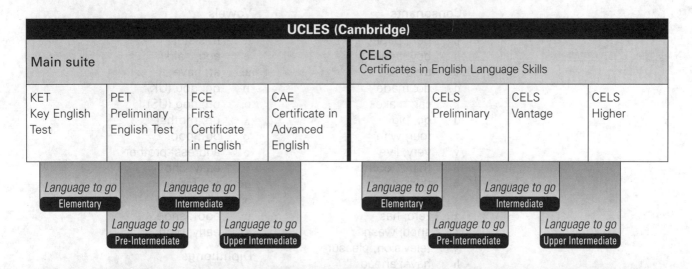

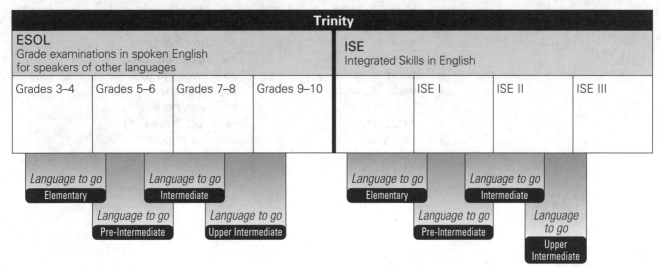

11

Phonemic symbols

The symbols in this chart represent the sounds used in standard British English and some of the most common variations in American English. We have used the symbols in the Teaching notes to help clarify pronunciation points dealt with in the lesson. We have not included them in the Students' Book, because we feel it is not always easy or practical to teach them on a short course or a course involving continuous enrolment.

However, you may find it useful to introduce certain symbols to students to help them with their individual pronunciation needs. If you do, we would recommend that you:
- only teach a few symbols at a time – little and often;
- get students to practise the sounds, but do not aim for perfection – a comprehensible approximation is good enough;
- relate the symbols to words which students already know.

The example words here are all taken from the Longman defining vocabulary of 2,000 words used in *The Longman Active Study Dictionary* and *The Longman Dictionary of Contemporary English*.

Consonants

p	pen; paper
b	boy; table
t	to; sit
d	do; made
k	car; make
g	go; big
f	four; wife
v	very; live
θ	think; tooth
ð	this; other
s	say; bus
z	zero; has
ʃ	shop; wash
ʒ	television; pleasure
h	have; ahead
tʃ	cheese; watch
dʒ	job; bridge
m	man; come
n	name; ten
ŋ	thing; singer
w	water; flower
l	late; yellow
r	run; carry
j	yes; you

Vowels

ɪ	it; sister
e	egg; said
æ	at; have
ɒ	on; dog (UK)
ɒː	on; dog (US)
ʌ	up; mother
ʊ	put; book
ə	address; brother
iː	easy; she
ɑː	art; father
ɔː	all; door
uː	boot; shoe
ɜː	early; work

Diphthongs

eɪ	able; wait
aɪ	I; buy
ɔɪ	toy; noise
əʊ	over; go (UK)
oʊ	over; go (US)
aʊ	out; town
ɪə	ear; here
eə	air; there (UK)
ʊə	sure; poor

Teaching notes

by Robin Wileman and Araminta Crace

Vocabulary Regular and irregular verbs
Grammar Past simple
Language to go Talking about past events

A life of achievement

Language notes

- Many of the most commonly used verbs in English are irregular. See the list of irregular verbs on page 6 of the Phrasebook. Encourage students to learn a few at a time, as they come up, and to learn them in groups as presented in the Phrasebook, rather than to learn long lists.
- At this level students often experiment with verbs in the past, and may 'invent' forms (e.g. ~~goed~~ [went]). It's also common for students to use the past form for negatives and questions, e.g. *We didn't ~~went~~ yesterday* [go], *What time did it started?*
- Focus on when to use the /ɪd/ ending as in *wanted* /wɒntɪd/ and *ended* /endɪd/. We feel it is not important to go into the small difference between /t/ and /d/ endings.

Way in

- Ask students to think of the person who they think has achieved most out of life. It could be a famous person or someone known personally to the student. You may want to give them an example of your own. In pairs, they tell each other about the person and why they think they have achieved so much.

Speaking

1 Practise forming questions and answers from the list, following the example given. You may wish to clarify some of the vocabulary in the questions, such as *married, apartment, musical instrument.*
 - Ask students to circulate and ask each other the questions until they find the right person, making a note of their answers.

2 Get a few students to report back to the class, following the example.

Reading

3 Get students to look at the photos of *Oprah Winfrey* and ask if they know who she is. Get them to tell the class anything they know about her.
 - You may wish to see if they know the answers to the three questions in bold in the text. Then ask them to read the texts to find out the answers.
 - Get them to look back at the list in Exercise 1. Then ask them to read the text and find the five things in the list that are true for Oprah Winfrey.

> She can act.
> She's got a car.
> She hasn't got any children.
> She enjoyed reading as a child.
> She lives in an apartment.

4 Ask students to look at Oprah Winfrey's lifeline. Briefly check that they understand the format, i.e. each point on the line should contain a year, and corresponds to one of the numbered sentences. Then get them to read the text again and fill in the missing dates.

> 1 1954
> 2 1973 (when she was 19)
> 3 1977
> 4 1984
> 5 1985
> 6 1997

Grammar focus

5 Ask students to look at the examples of the past simple in the table. You may want to reinforce the forms by writing your own table on the board.
 - Students read the sentence above the table, and discuss whether they think it is true or false. Check the answer with the whole class.

> True

6 CD Ask students to listen to the recording and repeat the regular past simple forms. Get them to pay attention to the pronunciation of the past simple endings /t/ /d/ /ɪd/.

Practice

7 Get students to read the text through.
 - Ask them which time period it refers to and elicit that it describes a daily routine.
 - Tell students they are going to write about Karl Jones's day yesterday, and ask which tense they should use.
 - If necessary, elicit the past tenses of some of the verbs, then get students to write out the passage in the past simple.

> 1 worked 2 started 3 had 4 gave 5 didn't want
> 6 didn't leave 7 What did he do...?

Get talking

8 Draw a lifeline on the board and put a few dates which were important in your own life, leaving space to write in the actual events. Then get students to ask you questions about one or two of the dates until they arrive at the correct answer, e.g. the day you graduated, got married, etc.
 - When students have got the idea from your example, ask them to draw their own lifeline on a piece of paper. Make sure they only include the important dates in their life, leaving a space for the actual events.
 - In pairs, get students to exchange papers and complete each other's lifelines by asking each other questions. Use the example in the book if necessary.
 - Ask them to report back to the class, following the example.

LESSON 2
Verb patterns

Vocabulary   Free time activities
Grammar   Likes / dislikes + -ing form + qualifying adverbs
Language to go   Saying how much you like doing things

Billy Elliot

Language notes

- Although it is possible for verbs such as *like*, *love* to be followed by either an *-ing* form or an infinitive, we feel it is important at this level to focus on the more 'neutral' and therefore more useful form, verb + *-ing* form, and not confuse students with the subtle differences between the two forms.
- Intonation is important when using qualifying adverbs, and it is worth spending a little time practising this, to get students pronouncing *really* in a very emphatic way, and *quite* in a much more tentative way, as on the recording.

Way in

- Write the names of some activities on separate cards. Ask a student to choose one of the cards and hand it to you. Read the card, then mime the activity, getting students to guess what you are doing. Then give a card to each student and get them to read their own card and take it in turns to mime it for the class. Get the other students to guess what the activity is. This could be done in pairs if you wish.

Vocabulary and speaking

1   Ask students to put the words into the correct columns, using the example if necessary. Explain that it is the nouns which need an accompanying verb, and that we would tend to use *play* for ball sports such as football and *do* for activities without a ball. (NB We also use *play* for games such as chess.)

> *verb only:* box, run, swim
> *play:* football, golf, volleyball
> *do:* gymnastics, yoga, ballet

2   Ask students to work with a partner and discuss the two questions. It's interesting to note differences between families and perhaps national cultures, but be careful not to make anyone feel 'put down' because their family or culture is 'different' in some way.

Reading

3   Students look at the photos; ask if anyone knows which film they come from (*Billy Elliot*), and if anyone has seen it. Pre-teach *strike* (noun and verb) (when workers stop working because they want more money or better conditions).

Background information

- *Billy Elliot* is set in a working-class mining town in the north of England during the miners' strike of the 1980s. The strike went on for some time and left many families in serious poverty.
- Based on real events, the film is a twist on the usual 'working-class boy makes good' theme. It is the story of how a boy turns his back on the traditional values and expectations of his family and background. Instead of training to be a boxer, he goes to ballet classes and becomes a successful ballet dancer. His father struggles to accept his son's decision but in the end the two are reconciled.

- Refer students back to the list of activities in Exercise 1. Then ask them to look at the questions and read the text quickly for the answers.

> 1 boxing, football, running, ballet
> 2 ballet

4   Ask students to look at the four sentences, then read the text again and complete them. Encourage them to discuss their answers together.

> 1 drinking / arguing
> 2 drinking / arguing / listening to rock music
> 3 listening to rock music / playing football / dancing
> 4 boxing / running

Grammar focus

5   Ask students to look at the examples from the text. Check that students understand the meanings of the adverbs and their position in the sentences.
- Ask them to underline the correct word in the two explanations.

> 1 *-ing* form
> 2 really

6    The main purpose of this listening activity is to practise the appropriate intonation. Ask students to listen and repeat the sentences using the correct intonation. Stop the recording between sentences to give students time to repeat.

Practice

7   Ask students to write sentences using the prompts, following the example. Remind them of the meaning of the symbols, as in the Grammar focus. Help them to position the adverbs and change the form of the verb correctly.

> 1 Felipe really loves going to football matches.
> 2 Sarah really hates playing volleyball.
> 3 Trevor and Simon don't enjoy watching TV very much.
> 4 Oscar quite enjoys boxing.
> 5 Paula doesn't like doing ballet very much.
> 6 I quite like doing yoga.
> 7 We really enjoy playing golf.

Get talking …

8   Ask students to fill in the column on the chart individually first, following the instructions given.
- In pairs, get them to ask each other questions so that they can complete the column for their partner. Remind them to use the suggested symbols and refer to the example if necessary.
- Get students to report their partner's preferences back to the class.
- Do a quick class survey to find out which activities are more popular with men and which with women.

… and writing

9   Help students to start writing a report of their survey results following the example given. If there is not enough time, ask students to finish their report for homework.

Vocabulary Clothes; weather and seasons
Grammar Present simple and present continuous
Language to go Comparing usual and present situations

Hurricane

Language notes

- It's common for students to use the present simple in English to describe something happening 'around now', e.g. ~~What do you do now? I have my lunch~~. What are you doing now? I'm having my lunch. Some languages don't have a present continuous form at all, and in some languages the present simple is used to describe things happening 'around now', where the present continuous would be used in English.
- It's important to point out those verbs which are normally used in the present simple, e.g. know, understand, but not to say that they can **never** be used in a continuous form.
- We can say It's 35 degrees Celsius or It's 35 degrees Centigrade or just It's 35 degrees. In the USA the Fahrenheit scale is used, and in the UK both Fahrenheit and Celsius are used. In most other countries, Celsius is the only scale used (see conversion table in the Phrasebook).

Way in

- Divide the class into pairs and tell them to make a list of all the clothes they are wearing today. Give them a time limit of three minutes.
- Draw the outline of a body on the board. When students tell you the names of their clothes, draw them in and label them, if you like.
- You may want to have two separate outlines for male and female clothes.

Vocabulary and speaking

1 Ask students to match the pictures of the seasons with the three best sentences in the list. Check and practise pronunciation of the seasons and words describing weather. Students may need help with minus /ˈmaɪnəs/ and the stress in degrees.
Point out: UK autumn; US fall.

Spring	It's eighteen degrees. It's quite warm. It's windy.
Summer	It's thirty-five degrees. It's really hot. It's sunny.
Autumn	It's twelve degrees; It's quite cool. It's raining.
Winter	It's minus thirty-two degrees. It's really cold. It's snowing.

2 Ask students to match the words in the box with the pictures. Check and practise pronunciation, particularly the difference between the vowel sounds in shorts /ʃɑːts/ and T-shirt /ˈtiːʃɜːt/.

hat G   gloves J   umbrella I   boots F   shorts A
T-shirt C   jacket L   sunhat K   scarf E   coat B
sandals H   sweater D

3 Get students to discuss the questions in pairs or small groups. Obviously they may have to make a guess at average temperatures, and shouldn't get bogged down in arguments, as the aim is simply to practise the vocabulary! The 'right' answer is not important. Ask them to report back and compare their answers with the class.

Listening

4 Ask students to describe the weather in the picture. Check they know that a *hurricane* /ˈhʌrɪkən/ is a violent storm with a strong, fast, circular wind. Find out if anybody in the class has ever experienced a hurricane or any other extreme weather conditions.
- Check that students know where the places are (refer to a map if possible) and ask students to pick the three places which suffer from hurricanes. Help by explaining that hurricanes are much more frequent in certain tropical areas.

The Dominican Republic, Miami, Puerto Rico

5 📖 Explain that students are going to listen to a news report about a hurricane as it is happening. Ask them to read the statements. Then get them to listen and decide if they are true or false.

1 False	2 True
3 False	4 False
5 True	6 False
7 True	8 True

Grammar focus

6 Ask students to look at the examples. You may wish to focus on the form of each tense, and give a table of the positive, negative and question forms on the board. Contrast the use of the auxiliary verbs *do* and *be*. Get students to complete the explanations, using the correct tense name.

1 present continuous   2 present simple
3 present simple

Practice

7 Ask students to fill the gaps in the sentences with the correct forms of the verbs. They could check their answers in pairs before class feedback.

1 know / doesn't usually have / is snowing / are staying
2 rains / is shining / are wearing / aren't carrying / do
3 think / wear
4 rains / have / is raining / is wearing
5 gets / doesn't get

Get writing ...

8 Get students to think about possible differences in weather between their country and the USA.
- Ask students to read the e-mail from J and consider how they might answer the questions.
- Then ask students to reply to the e-mail, making sure they answer each question and offer suitable advice. If all the students are writing about the same country, they could do this in pairs.
- You may wish to use the photocopiable models in the Writing bank (page 146) to focus on the conventions of e-mail writing.

... and talking

9 In pairs, ask students to compare e-mails and see if their advice is the same as their partner's. Then ask some pairs to report back to the class.

Vocabulary   Possessions
Grammar   Possessive 's, possessive adjectives / pronouns, *belong to*
Language to go   Talking about what belongs to us

Possessions we hate

Language notes

- It's common (and understandable) for students to confuse pronouns: *It's ~~him~~ book* [*his*]; *that's ~~she~~ guitar.* [*her*]. There may also be interference from languages where the possessive adjectives can have a 'plural' form: *They are ~~hers~~ friends* [*her*]. It's much better at this level to use exemplification and practice than grammatical terminology.
- There may also be confusion between *its* and *it's*, and *who / who's / whose?*
- With the verb *belong to*, it's important to emphasise the order of 'thing owned + belong to + owner'. Many students will want to reverse the construction, e.g. *~~I belong to it~~*, [*It belongs to me*] because of influence from a similar verb in their language.

Way in

- Bring a collection of your own possessions to the class, e.g. wallet, keys, diary, glasses, pens, mobile phone. Take them from your bag or pocket and show them to the class. Check that they know the words, and tell them that they are your *possessions*. Check pronunciation of *possessions* /pə'zeʃənz/.
- Tell students which two possessions you can't live without. Ask them to do the same in pairs, followed by brief feedback from one or two pairs.

Vocabulary and speaking

1   Ask students to look at the pictures and elicit / check pronunciation of the items.
- Get them to work alone and to rank the possessions in order of importance from 1–8.
- In pairs, ask them to compare their answers and see if they agree.

2   Ask students to look at the columns and the example words. Remind them that all these words are spelt with the letter '*a*', but they are all pronounced differently. Check that they are aware of the different pronunciations: /mæn/ /wɒt/ /kɑː/ /'sɔfə/ /deɪ/.
- Play the recording, stopping after each word to give students time to write.

man	what	car	sofa	day
camera	watch	guitar	musical instrument	radio
laptop				mini-disk player

3   Teach or revise the meaning of *to irritate* /'ɪrɪteɪt/ – to annoy a little.
- Put students into small groups to discuss which possessions irritate them. Encourage them to give reasons.

Reading and listening

4   Ask students to look at the two questions then read the text quickly to find the answers.
- Elicit or revise the word *guest*.
- Discuss whether they have a similar show in their own countries.

1 The room containing the thing which frightens each person the most.
2 The guests bring things they hate and want to put in Room 101.

5   Tell students they are going to hear a recording of the Room 101 TV programme. The interviewer is a man and he is speaking to Andrea about her choices for Room 101.
- Ask students to look at the three questions. Then ask them to listen for the answers.
- Let students discuss their answers before you do the class feedback.

1 a guitar, a mobile phone, a TV
2 the guitar and the TV
3 the TV presenter

6   Ask students to listen again for who each of the possessions belongs to.

It's *her brother's* guitar.
It's *her* (mobile) phone.
It's *her parents'* TV.

Grammar focus

7   Ask students to look at the table.
- Draw on the board a pin man labelled 'Paul' and a guitar. Write the first sentence on the board: *It's Paul's guitar.* Cross out *Paul's* and elicit what other word could go there (*his*). Then cross out *guitar* to show the use of the pronoun, and elicit the sentence *It belongs to him.* If necessary you could repeat this with the other examples in the table.
- Build up a list of the other pronouns on the board, or refer students to the Grammar reference for this lesson.
- Tell students that the sentences in the table are all answers to one question, (a) or (b). Ask them to discuss in pairs which question it is, then check with the class.

b Whose is it?

Practice

8   Ask students to rewrite the sentences, following the example.

1 The mini-disk player belongs to Anna. / It belongs to Anna.
2 It's David's video camera.
3 The TV is ours. / It's ours.
4 It's John's mobile phone.
5 It's theirs. / The radio is theirs.
6 It's her watch.
7 It's Katy's camera.
8 It belongs to Daniel. / The laptop belongs to Daniel.

Get talking

9   First students decide individually upon three possessions for Room 101; one of their own and two for family or friends. Remind students that they should be objects they hate.
- Ask them to think about reasons for their choices.
- Then get them to discuss these with a partner.
- The listener decides what can go into Room 101 – with reasons.
- If time, have a quick class discussion to find out if a lot of people wanted to put the same things into Room 101.

Vocabulary Weddings
Grammar *Should / shouldn't* and imperatives
Language to go Giving advice

A Scottish wedding

Language notes
- Both *should* and the imperative can sound too abrupt if they are over emphasised, so encourage students to use polite intonation with imperatives, and to stress the main verb not *should*.
- As this is the first lesson in the 'modals' strand, you may wish to point out that the verb *should* is a modal auxiliary, and so does not need an auxiliary itself, e.g. *You ~~don't should~~ wear a hat* [*shouldn't*].
- Students may need to be reminded that *advice* is an uncountable noun and so has no plural and does not take the third person *s*: *I need some ~~advices~~* [*advice*].

Way in
- Write 'United Kingdom' on the board and ask students what they know about it. Don't spend too long on this!

Background information
England, Wales and Scotland together are called Britain or Great Britain. The United Kingdom, or the UK, is made up of Great Britain and Northern Ireland. The Republic of Ireland is southern Ireland, a separate country.
All four countries are governed centrally by the UK parliament in London, but three of them also have a form of independent government: the Welsh Assembly, the Scottish Parliament, and, at the time of writing, the Northern Ireland Assembly.
Scotland is probably the most 'independent' of the three countries, with its own legal system, education system, and the power to collect taxes.
English is spoken throughout the UK, but there are also the Welsh and Irish languages, and some Gaelic is spoken in Scotland.

- In small groups, ask students to think of five things that they know about Scotland. Then ask them to share their ideas with the class.

Background information
- Scotland is famous for *tartan*, a woollen material with squares of different colours and patterns. Each pattern historically belongs to one *clan*, or family.
- *Kilts* are made of tartan. These are traditional skirts worn by men, usually on special occasions. (See picture on page 12 in the Students' Book.)
- Scotland has many lakes, called *lochs*. (See picture on page 12.)
- The Loch Ness Monster is thought to live in Loch Ness, but nobody has ever proved it!
- *Bagpipes* are a famous Scottish musical instrument. (See picture on page 12.)
- Scotland is famous for its whisky, called Scotch.

Vocabulary
1 Use the picture to teach and revise wedding vocabulary.
- Ask students to fill in the gaps in the sentences, following the example.

1 bride 2 bridesmaids 3 guests 4 reception
5 best man 6 honeymoon

Listening
2 🔊 Explain that students are going to listen to part of an American radio show. The guest, Rory Graham, is going to give advice to listeners who phone in.
- Ask students to read the questions and then listen to find the answers.

1 to a traditional wedding in Scotland
2 what to do, what to wear and what present to take

3 Ask students to read the five pieces of advice. Then get them to listen again and mark whether the advice is true or false.

1 False   2 False   3 True   4 True   5 True

Grammar focus
4 Ask students to read the examples in the table.
- You could write *I should* on the board, and elicit from students how to make this negative – write *I shouldn't*. Point out that there is no auxiliary verb *do* or *be*. Then elicit the question form and write *Should I?* on the board, again highlighting there is no need for an auxiliary. You could then add a verb, e.g. *I should go*, and point out that *should* is actually an auxiliary itself.
- Students repeat the examples, to practise unstressed *should* with the main verb stressed, and stressing the imperative form of the verbs.
- Students complete sentences 1 and 2.

1 It is …   2 It isn't …

Practice
5 Ask students to fill in the gaps with the correct form of *should* and the verb, following the example.

1 B: … he definitely *shouldn't see* the bride.
2 A: How *should* a French couple *go* from … ?
   B: They *should walk*.
3 A: … *should* you *give* just one … ?
   B: You *should give* a present …
4 A: … you *shouldn't dance* first.
   B: Why *should* you *do* that?
   A: Because the newly married couple *should* dance first.

6 Put students into pairs to practise the dialogues.

Get talking …
7 Divide the class into groups.
- Ask the groups to make notes as they discuss the suggested topics listed.
- Ask them to decide on five pieces of advice to give. Encourage them to give reasons for their choice.

… and writing
8 Ask students to continue from the example given. They can complete the letters in class or for homework.
- You may wish to use the photocopiable model in the Writing bank (page 147) to focus on the conventions of writing an informal letter.

Vocabulary	Countries and continents
Grammar	The future with *going to*
Language to go	Talking about future plans

Travel with English

Language notes

- Some students may want to use *will* during this lesson, as they see *will* as 'the future' in English. This lesson focuses on the use of *going to* when we have already decided on a plan, whereas *will* is only used when a decision is made at the time of speaking.
  e.g. *I'm going to take the first train to London tomorrow. So am I. We'll get a taxi to the station together then.* The two forms are dealt with in contrast in Lesson 26.
- You may want to spend some time on the weak form /tə/ e.g. *I'm going to visit the Inuits.* Before a vowel sound, however, the vowel sound in *to* is strong: /tuː/ e.g. *I'm going to arrive at ten o'clock.*

Way in

- Ask students how many continents there are, and brainstorm them: *Africa, Europe, Asia, Australasia (also called Oceania), Antartica, North America,* and *South America.*
- Have a quick class quiz. Ask students, for example:
  1 Which is the biggest continent?
  2 Which is the smallest?
  3 Which has most people?
  4 Where do the people live longest?

1 Asia – 44,614,000 square kilometres
2 Australasia – 8,000,000 square kilometres
3 Asia
4 Australasia – men 75.4 and women 81.1 years on average

Vocabulary and speaking

1 Ask students to describe the pictures and see if they can identify the countries shown.
- Get students to read through the travel article very quickly to pick out the five country names only. Give a time limit of one minute. Then ask them to match the names of the countries to the continents.
- Check their answers and see if they guessed correctly from looking at the pictures.

Africa – South Africa
Europe – Ireland
Asia – India
Australasia – Australia
America – Canada

2 📖 Check that students understand what the stress patterns mean. Explain that the boxes represent the number of syllables. The biggest boxes represent the syllable with the main stress.
- Play the recording and get students to repeat the intonation.
- Ask them to put each country in the correct stress group.
- Stop the recording after each country to give students time to think and to write.
- You may want to remind students to mark in the word stress when storing new vocabulary.

Pattern 1: Poland, Ireland
Pattern 2: Italy, India, Canada
Pattern 3: Colombia, Australia, South Africa

3 Think of the name of a country which has not yet been mentioned. Tell the class the reasons that you would like to visit this country.
- In pairs, get students to discuss which country they would most like to visit and why.
- Have a quick class discussion to see which is the most popular country and why.

Reading

4 Get students to read the text and complete the table.

	When to visit	What to see/do
Australia	December	Outdoor life, Sydney water sports
South Africa	February	safaris, beaches
India	January	Look at views, visit monuments and markets
Canada	November	Look at views/mountains/lakes
Ireland	March	St Patrick's Day festivities City life and countryside

Grammar focus

5 Ask students to look at the examples in the table. You may want to highlight the positive, negative and question forms on the board, as this construction is quite complex.
- Then students discuss in pairs whether the statement is true or false.

True

Practice

6 Ask students to complete the sentences. Do the example with the class before they start.

1 Laura *is going to see* beautiful monuments in India.
2 We *are going to walk* by the lakes in Canada.
3 *Are we going to swim* in the sea in South Africa?
4 I *am going to visit* Alice Springs and other famous places in Australia.
5 Alex *is going to take part* in the St Patrick's Day festivities in Ireland.
6 They *aren't going to stay* in luxury accommodation in South Africa.
7 *Are you going to climb* any mountains in Canada?
8 She *isn't going to travel* to Australia in July when the weather is cold.

Get talking

7 Students look at the article again.
- Divide the class into groups so that they can compare their choices and the reasons behind them.
- Ask them to vote and reach a group decision. Then get them to discuss their plans for when they arrive.
- Ask the groups to share their decisions with the class.

LESSON **7**

Adjectives

Vocabulary Adjectives to describe character
Grammar Comparatives
Language to go Making comparisons

Why women iron

Language notes

- Though the concept of comparatives is fairly straightforward, the form is potentially difficult. Confusion between the two types of construction (*more ... than* and *not as ... as*) can lead to errors such as ~~He is taller as me,~~ [*He is taller than me*] and ~~He is not as tall than me.~~ [*He is not as tall as me*]. It's also common for students to apply the 'wrong' rule when forming comparative adjectives, e.g. ~~She is more strong than him~~ [*stronger*] or ~~He is aggressiver than me.~~ [*more aggressive*]
- Pronunciation: this language provides a useful opportunity to focus on linking, i.e. the 'joining together' of two words, from consonant to vowel e.g. *strong as* /strɒŋəz/, and from vowel to consonant, e.g. *stronger than* /strɒŋgəðən/. Raising students' awareness of points like this will help their comprehension of spoken English as much as their own pronunciation. Don't be too insistent that students come out with perfect linking every time – they don't need to!
- The topic of this lesson may well provoke some lively debate, but the tone should be kept fairly lighthearted and you may need to be careful that the more vociferous or opinionated students don't get on a soapbox and take over! To ensure that everyone is comfortable contributing, it's important that neither the book nor the teacher should be seen as taking one 'side' or the other.

Way in

- Write the lesson title *Why women iron* on the board. Check that students understand the verb *iron* /aɪən/, and ask students if they agree that only women iron, and if so why they think that is. You could broaden the discussion out to include other household tasks such as washing up or cooking.

Vocabulary and speaking

1 Ask the students to underline the correct adjective. Do the first one as an example with the class. Tell students not to worry if they aren't sure about some. Let them check in pairs, then go through the answers, clarifying where necessary.

1 messy	2 talkative	3 cooperative
4 tidy	5 competitive	6 aggressive

2 Students describe the photos in pairs, to practise some of the new vocabulary. Ask them to report to the class some of the things they said; check they understand the words by asking why they chose them, e.g. *I think the rugby players are aggressive because they are playing hard against the other team.*

There are no hard and fast answers, but students may well say that the rugby players are hardworking, cooperative (with their team), aggressive and competitive (against the other team), and that the father and child are talkative, hardworking, messy, cooperative.

Reading

3 Ask students to decide which of the adjectives most suit men or women. You could get them to mark the adjective *M* for 'men' or *W* for 'women'.
- Emphasise that this is a discussion and there are NO correct answers!

4 Ask students to read the text to discover if their answers are the same as the text.

According to the article, characteristics more typical of:
Boys / men: messy, competitive, aggressive
Girls / women: hardworking, talkative, tidy, cooperative.

5 Students read the questions. Check that they understand them. Then they read, and check their answers.

1 That they are taught their behaviour by society.
2 That they should change their behaviour.
3 No. They think men and women are born with different behaviour and you can't really change this.

Grammar focus

6 Students look at the examples in the table and complete explanations 1–4 with endings a–d.

1d 2c 3a 4b

Practice

7 Students rewrite the sentences following the example. The sentences may provoke discussion, but tell students that they will have an opportunity to discuss them in the 'Get talking' later in the lesson.

1 *Girls aren't as* <u>fast as boys</u>.
2 *Boys are* <u>noisier than girls</u>.
3 *Women are* <u>more talkative than men</u>.
4 *Men aren't as* <u>tidy as women</u>.
5 *Men are* <u>messier than women</u>.
6 *Schoolboys aren't as* <u>hardworking as schoolgirls</u>.
7 *Girls aren't as* <u>good as boys at football</u>.

8 Students listen and check their answers to Exercise 7.

9 Ask the class to listen and repeat what they hear.
- Stop after each sentence to give students time to repeat. Focus on linking from vowel to consonant: /strɒŋgəðən/, and from consonant to vowel: /aːntəzˈstrɒŋəz/.

Get talking

10 First ask students to do the questionnaire individually.
- Then divide the class into small groups, preferably mixed male and female, and ask them to discuss their opinions.
- Encourage them to give reasons and finish with a quick class discussion. (Be prepared to calm the discussion down if it becomes too heated!)

Present perfect

Vocabulary	Adventure sports
Functions	Present perfect and past simple
Language to go	Talking about past experiences

Take a risk

Language notes

• The use of the present perfect to express 'experience' is not difficult but students often use it to talk about past events at a specific time, e.g. ~~I've played~~ basketball when I was a student [I played...]. In terms of form, there is the use of *have* as an auxiliary, and the irregular past participles for students to learn.

Way in

• Elicit the names of sports from students. This could be done in the form of a competition: in teams, students have one minute to come up with as many sports as possible. They then write them on the board (or read them out) in lists, and score one point for each sport not mentioned by any other team.

Vocabulary

1
  • Ask students to look at the pictures. Explain that these are known as 'extreme sports', and briefly ask if anyone has done any of them.
  • Students match the pictures to the words.

1 rock climbing A	4 snowboarding E
2 scuba diving F	5 skateboarding D
3 windsurfing B	

2 Play the recording. Stop the recording after each sport and get students to repeat each word.
  • Check that students understand what the stress patterns mean. Remind them that the boxes represent the number of syllables. The biggest boxes represent the syllable with the main stress.
  • Ask them to put each sport in the correct stress group.

water skiing, scuba diving
rock climbing, windsurfing, snowboarding, skateboarding

Listening

3 Ask students to look at the photos from the brochure, and discuss whether they would like to go on such a holiday, and why.
  • Tell students that they are going to listen to some people who are on the Adventure Zone holiday.
  • Ask them to listen and decide if the statements are true or false.

1 True   2 False

4 Ask students to look at the table.
  • Explain that Andy has been waterskiing, so there is a tick in that column, and that he enjoyed it, so there is a tick there. Check they understand that a tick (✓) means 'yes' and a cross (✗) means 'no'.
  • Students listen again and complete the table.

	waterskiing		windsurfing		scuba diving		rock climbing	
	yes	enjoyed	yes	enjoyed	yes	enjoyed	yes	enjoyed
Andy	✓	✓	✗	-	✗	-	✓	✗
Paula	✓	✓	✓	✓	✓	✓	✓	✓

5 Ask students to try and choose the correct verb form before listening again. Then play the tape again.

Dave: *Have you ever done ...?*
Andy: *I've played ... / I've been ...*
Dave: When *did you do ...?*
Dave: And what *did you think ...?*
Andy: *I really enjoyed ...*

Grammar focus

6 Students look at the examples in the table. You may wish to focus on:
  – the form of ...
  – the irregular ...
  – *been* and *gone* ...
  • Get students to complete the explanations by filling in the spaces.

1 present perfect   2 past simple   3 present perfect

Practice

7 Get students to complete the sentences with the correct form of the present perfect or past simple, following the example.

1 A: Have you ever played ... ?   B: haven't
2 A: Did you watch ... ?   B: did / was
3 A: Has your sister ever run ... ?   B: hasn't / ran
4 A: Did you enjoy ... ?   B: didn't / was
5 A: have ('ve) never done   B: went
  A: Did you like .... ?   B: had

8 Ask students to work with a partner and practise the dialogues. Listen to them and correct any mistakes with the two tenses.

Get talking ...

9 Ask students to choose four dangerous sports and make questions on a chart starting: *Have you ever...?*

Get them to include space on their chart to find out who enjoyed these sports, who hated them, who has only watched them, who wants to try them again and what other sports they have done.
Then students walk around the room and ask the questions, filling in the answers on the chart. Finish with a brief class feedback.

... and writing

10 Tell the class to imagine they are going on an Adventure Zone holiday. Ask them to write a paragraph on their application form about their adventure sports experiences.

Reassure them that, if they have no adventure sports experience, they can use their imagination.
If time is limited, let students do this for homework.
You may wish to use the photocopiable models in the Writing bank (pages 148 and 149) to focus on the conventions of writing a formal letter of application and filling in an application form.

Vocabulary   At the office: verb + noun combinations
Function   Offers and requests
Language to go   Making and responding to offers and requests

Job share

Language notes
- Polite and friendly intonation can be more important than using the correct form when making requests.
- When making an offer it is common for students to use the present simple rather than the future simple, e.g. ~~I help~~ not *I'll help*. This could be because students may use the present simple to make offers in their language. But also it can be quite difficult for students to hear the contracted form *'ll*, the usual form in offers, so they may mistake it for the present simple.

Way in
- Brainstorm a list of jobs with the students. Write them up on the board. In pairs, ask students to choose one job and discuss the daily tasks which may be involved in each of these jobs. Get them to report back to the class. If there is time, you could discuss which jobs and which kinds of tasks they prefer.

Vocabulary
1   Get students to complete the sentences, following the example. This exercise presents some useful collocations; encourage students to record collocations as a word group (e.g. *leave a message*, *send a fax*, *sign your name*) rather than as single words.

1 got	5 make
2 leave	6 had, made
3 arrange	7 do
4 do	8 sign

Reading and speaking
2   Get students to look at the four photos and discuss in pairs the daily tasks involved in the work of the four people. You may want to check pronunciation of the jobs.

Example answers
Taxi driver – drive, take money, talk to passengers, clean taxi.
Musician – practise alone, rehearse with others, clean and look after instrument, travel to concerts, perform.
Teacher – prepare lessons, give lessons, mark work, discuss work with pupils/parents.
Secretary – answer the phone, type letters, make phone calls, send faxes.

- Now get them to read the article and discuss the two questions in pairs, then as a class.

Possible answers
1 It could be argued that all four jobs could be shared, though that of the professional musician might be the most difficult to share, given that a high professional standard is required, and probably regular rehearsals which both job sharers would have to attend.
2 Lack of continuity for the employer, client or pupil; possible feelings of resentment if one person feels they are working harder than the other person; possible disputes over division of tasks between the two job sharers.

- Ask students to decide whether they could share their own job, or a job they would like to do. Get them to think of the advantages and disadvantages.

Listening
3   Set the context and check students understand *model agency*.
- Ask them to read the questions and then listen to find the answers.

1 Secretaries / personal assistants to Mr Davis.
2 Ken has to do Pat's jobs and his own.

4   Ask students to read the sentences before listening again, then mark them *T* or *F*. Get them to check answers with a partner before class feedback. This will give them some extra speaking practice.

1 True   2 False   3 False   4 True
5 False (he wanted Pat to do it)   6 False

Language focus
5   Ask the students to look at the examples in the table and answer the questions. Focus on the use of *can* and *could* for requests, and the use of *will* / *'ll* in positive offers, but *shall* in the question form.

1 examples 1 and 2
2 examples 3 and 4

6   Stop the recording after each sentence to give students time to repeat.
Remind students to use *polite* intonation, following the model on the recording.

Practice
7   Get students to complete the dialogues, following the example and using the verbs in brackets.

1 A: Shall I phone ... ?
  B: Can / Could you book ... ?
2 A: Can / Could you write ... ?
  B: I'll give ...
3 A: I'll arrange ...
  B: Can / could you send ... ?
4 A: Shall I order ... ?
  B: Can / Could you check ... ?

8   Students practise the completed dialogues in pairs.

Get talking
9   In pairs, ask the class to rewrite the dialogues, following the example.

Example answers
A: Can / Could you send this fax to Peter Fox, please?
B: Sorry, I'm afraid the fax machine is broken.
A: Can / Could you send him an e-mail then?
B: Can / Could you give me his e-mail address?
A: Here you are.
B: Can / Could you tell me what to write?
A: Can / Could you ask him to come to the Friday meeting? Can / Could you book a restaurant for Friday evening for ten people?
B: OK, I'll book a table at the Lemon Tree restaurant.

- Students read the revised dialogues aloud in pairs.
- Finally, encourage them to try *without* books.

Vocabulary	Verbs and their opposites
Grammar	Zero conditional (*if* + present form + present form)
Language to go	Talking about consequences

Behave yourself

Language notes

- It can be useful for students to learn and to store verbs in pairs of opposites, and to note down how the verb operates in a sentence, i.e. whether it is followed by an *-ing* form or an infinitive, the order of the direct and indirect objects, etc.
- Students who have studied conditional forms before may well request a full 'rundown' of all the conditional forms. The first and second conditional are covered later in the book, and it's probably best to resist dealing with them at this stage, to avoid overloading students.
- It's common for speakers of some languages to use *when* instead of *if* in conditional sentences; in fact with the zero conditional this isn't usually a problem, as *if* is very similar in meaning to *when* in zero conditional sentences.
- Point out that the 'zero' conditional is used to talk about things which the speaker sees as 'always' true.

Way in

- Ask students to tell you the opposite of a random selection of words, e.g. *yes–no*, *sit–stand*, *hot–cold*, etc. This could be done as a game, to see who comes up with the opposite first. Then students could play the game themselves in pairs or small groups.

Vocabulary

1 Ask students to match the verbs with their opposites, following the example. Some of them may have come up already in the 'Way in'.

give / take	come / go	fill / empty
lend / borrow	push / pull	remember / forget

2 Ask students to underline the correct verb, following the example.
- Remind them to think about both meaning *and* form.

1 give	2 lend	3 filled	4 remembered	5 forget
6 pulled				

Reading and speaking

3 You may need to check / revise vocabulary in the questionnaire, e.g. *trolley, refuse, cancel*.
- Ask students to do the quiz *individually* and discourage students from looking at each other's answers.
- Let them check the answer key.

4 Put the class into pairs and ask them to guess how their partner answered the questionnaire.
- Then get them to take turns to ask and answer the questions.
- Finally, let them look at the key, and decide who behaves better.

Grammar focus

5 Ask students to look at the examples in the table. Focus on the use of present tenses in both clauses, and the fact that a comma is not used when the result clause comes first.
- Students underline the correct words to complete the explanation. You may want to reinforce this with concept questions such as *Do I forget my friend's birthday? And then what do I do?*

The result depends on the *if* clause.

Practice

6 Ask students to complete the sentences using the verb in brackets, following the example.

1 doesn't start
2 The weather is bad / do you drive?
3 gets / pulls
4 doesn't come / phones
5 don't have / borrow
6 ask / does he lend

Get talking and writing

7 In pairs, ask students to think of three more questions to go into the questionnaire.
- If students are short on ideas, you may want to give some suggestions, e.g. *shops*: pushing to the front of the queue, not saying anything when a shop assistant gives you too much change; *restaurants*: shouting and complaining at waiters, talking loudly on a mobile phone; *family situations*: not washing up your own cups and plates, watching only what *you* want to watch on TV, etc.
- Get them to write out each of the questions, starting with *If…*, and also three alternative answers. You could do one pair's first idea as an example for the class.
- Finally, students turn to a new partner, ask their three questions and answer their partner's three questions.
- Ask a few students to report back to the class.

Vocabulary Customs: verb + noun combinations
Grammar *Used to / didn't use to*
Language to go Talking about past customs

Customs change

Language notes

- At this level it's best just to focus on the verb *used to*, e.g. *I used to live alone*, and not to contrast it with the adjectival form *be used to*, e.g. *I am used to living alone*.
- It's common for students to write the negative and question forms in the same way as the positive: *I used to work there. I didn't ~~used to~~ work there. Did you ~~used to~~ work there [use to]?*
- Sometimes students want to use *used to* instead of *usually* to describe present habits, as there may be a corresponding verb in their language which can be used in both past and present: *I'm enjoying learning English. I ~~used to~~ come to this class every day [I usually ...].*
- It's worth spending a little time on the pronunciation practice in Exercise 6, to get students working towards linking the two words *used* and *to*, and producing the more natural-sounding unvoiced consonants in *used* and weak form in *to*, i.e. /ˈjuːstə/. They will often want to use the 'normal' pronunciation of the verb *use*, voicing the *s* and over-emphasising the vowels, i.e. /juːzedtuː/.

Way in

Either:

- Brainstorm different types of footwear with the class. Pairs make a list, then feed back with the whole class. Don't get too bogged down in all the different kinds; try to keep to the most common footwear, e.g. *shoes, boots, sandals, slippers, trainers* (UK) / *sneakers* (US), *football boots, running shoes*. You could take this opportunity to pre-teach *high heels, platform shoes* for the reading text in the lesson.

Or:

- Ask pairs to think about how life today is different from life 100 years ago, where you come from. Have some class feedback, but let students use the past simple rather than trying to get them to use *used to*.

Vocabulary and speaking

1 Apart from the main aim of teaching the verb–noun collocations, this exercise and the following one are intended to start students thinking about how life may be different today and in the past.
   - Ask students to complete the questions with verbs from the box. Tell them they all make typical combinations. Show them the first one as an example.

1 wear	2 have	3 lock	4 wear
5 play	6 stay	7 take off / put on	

2 Students ask and answer the questions in Exercise 1 in pairs, referring to people and families they know. Encourage them to discuss whether their answers would be the same 20, 50 or 100 years ago.

Reading

3 Get students to briefly describe the pictures in pairs first, with some feedback to the class. If you haven't already done so in the 'Way in' use the pictures to check / pre-teach *sandals, high heels, platform shoes*.
   - Students read the article and match the paragraphs with the pictures.

1 C	2 A	3 D	4 E	5 B

4 Ask students to read the four statements. Then get them to read the article again and decide if the statements are true or false, following the example.

1 False
2 True
3 False
4 False

Grammar focus

5 Students look at the examples of *used to* in contrast to the past simple. You could focus on the form at this stage.
   - Ask students to underline the correct words in the explanations.

1 doesn't happen
2 only once

6 🔲 Ask students to listen to the sentences from Exercise 5.
   - Stop the tape after each sentence to give students time to repeat.
   - Encourage students to say *used to* as one linked item, and to stress the first syllable, which will help them produce the weak form of *to*.

Practice

7 Ask the students to complete the sentences with the correct words from the box, following the example.

Remind students to think about the spelling of *used* or *use*.

1 Did men use to open ... ?
2 didn't use to eat
3 Did you use to wear ... ?
4 didn't use to go
5 used to wear
6 Did your parents use to play ... ?

Get talking

8 First get students to look at the photos and say where / when they think the photos were taken.
   - In pairs, students use the photos to describe the past customs in the places in the photos, using *used to*.
   - Students may not have a lot to say in step 2, if they don't know much about the past history of their area. Encourage them to speculate a little, using *I think ... used to ...* and *Maybe ... used to...*
   - In step 3, students could talk about either their region or town, or specifically about life in their own family. Have some feedback to the class afterwards.

Vocabulary Shops and purchases
Grammar *Because, for* and infinitive of purpose (with *to*)
Language to go Giving reasons

Win some, lose some

Language notes
- It's common for students at this level to make the mistake of using *because* or *for* with the infinitive of purpose, e.g. *I went to the café for to get a coffee.* Draw attention to the different forms and give extra practice if necessary.
- Although there are three different pronunciations of plural endings /s/ /z/ and /ɪz/, the focus in Exercise 3 is mainly between /s/ and /ɪz/. Encourage students to make a note of the plural of new items as they go along.

Way in
- Ask students to think of their favourite shop and tell their partner about it. *What kind of shop is it? What's it called? Where is it? Why do you like it?* Use this activity to revise the names of different shops. If necessary, tell the students about your favourite shop as an example.

Vocabulary and speaking
1 Read out the list of places, drawing attention to pronunciation, especially convenience /kənˈviːnɪənts/ store and chemist's /ˈkeməsts/. NB a convenience store is a shop where you can buy food, alcohol, magazines, etc. It is often open 24 hours a day.
   Students match the photographs with the names of the shops, following the example.

   1 C   2 F   3 D   4 B   5 E   6 G

2 In groups, ask students to look at the list and discuss where the items can be obtained. Encourage them to help each other with difficult vocabulary.
   Go through the answers and use concept questions like *What's your favourite perfume?* or *What do you use matches for?* to check understanding. You may also want to revise countable and uncountable nouns at this point.

   Café: (a) cup of coffee, sandwiches, crisps
   Hairdresser's: (a) haircut, a wash and blow dry
   Convenience store: toothbrushes, a newspaper, matches, a can of beer, sandwiches, crisps, cigarettes
   Newsagent's: (a) newspaper, matches, crisps, cigarettes
   Restaurant: a can of beer, sandwiches, matches
   Clothes shop: socks, a T-shirt, sunglasses, clothes
   Chemist: medicine, perfume, toothbrushes

3 Remind students that we usually make plurals in English by adding 's' or 'es'. Say 'grapes' and ask if students can hear an /s/, /z/ or /ɪz/ sound at the end. (Answer /s/). Repeat with 'bananas' /z/ and 'oranges' /ɪz/.
   - Stop the recording after each word to give students time to repeat, then write it in the correct column.

/s/ /z/	/ɪz/
socks	sandwiches
cigarettes	toothbrushes
crisps	matches
clothes	sunglasses

   - Ask students why some plural endings are pronounced /ɪz/ (because the noun ends in /s/, /z/ or /ɪz/).

Reading and listening
4 Focus attention on the article *Double or quits* /kwɪts/. Make sure students read the questions and understand what they have to do, before reading the article itself.

   1 b   2 b

5 Check that students understand that they are now going to listen to Sarah (the woman in the article) talking about when she played the shopping game *Double or quits*.
   - Play the recording for students to discover if Sarah made more money, or not.

   She had more money at the end.

6 Play the recording again for students to match the places with the amount of money she has at each place.

   1 d   2 f   3 a   4 c   5 g   6 b   7 e

Grammar focus
7 Draw a stick person (Liz) on the board, with a thought bubble showing a cup of coffee. Next to it, draw a café. Ask 'What does Liz want?' (a cup of coffee). 'Where is she going?' (the café) 'Why is she going to the café?' (**Because** she wants a coffee / **for** a coffee / **to get** a coffee, etc.). Write correct suggestions on the board before asking students to look at the examples on page 27. Students then complete the explanations and check with a partner.

   1 for
   2 because
   3 the infinitive of purpose

Practice
8 Get students to rewrite the sentences, using the structures suggested in the brackets.
   - Students do the activity and check with a partner.

   1 He phoned the dentist for an appointment.
   2 He joined the club to make new friends.
   3 They bought some meat for dinner.
   4 I stopped at the garage because I wanted to buy or needed some petrol.
   5 We bought some paint to paint the chairs.
   6 I bought some stamps for my stamp album.
   7 She came into the living room because she wanted to get a chair.
   8 They went to the sports centre to play badminton.

Get talking
9 Before playing the game, double or quits, ask students to complete the form individually. Help with vocabulary if needed, and tell them prices can be approximate.
   - Divide the class into pairs and ask them to ask and answer the questions.
   - Remind students of the rules of the game. Students then take it in turns to throw a coin to see if they pay double, or pay nothing. Their partner should make a note of how much money they have won or lost.
   - At the end, find out who has the most/least money.

Vocabulary   Large numbers; hotel facilities
Grammar   *Have* and *have got*
Language to go   Facilities and regular activities

The Ritz

Language notes

- There is a lot of overlap between the use of *have got* and *have* when talking about possessions. *Have* is generally used in American English. *Have got* is preferred in British spoken English, e.g. *I've got a dog called Pooch*. Point out that *have / has* is usually contracted, and also that it's slightly more informal.
- This lesson provides an opportunity to practise writing and saying numbers in their different forms. Remind students there is no 's' when we say an exact number before hundred / thousand / million, e.g. *five hundred people, two thousand years, three million dollars*. Note we say *Millions of people*.
- In large numbers, we say *and* before the last two numbers: 2,345 = *two thousand, three hundred AND forty-five*. If the last number is less than ten, we use *and* before the last number, e.g. 2,304 = *two thousand, three hundred AND four*. Note there is no *and* in the following: 1,500 = *one thousand, five hundred*.
- In money, a pound or dollar sign comes before the amount, e.g. *£4.50; $9.99* (but we say *four pounds fifty, nine dollars ninety-nine*).

Way in

- Write *luxury hotel* on the board and check understanding of the word *luxury*. In pairs, students think of things a luxury hotel should have. Set a time limit and, at the end, ask the class to help you make a list of the features they would expect. Write (or draw pictures of) any new vocabulary on the board.

Vocabulary

1   ▭ Focus attention on the numbers in the box.
   - Tell students to listen to the recording and tick the numbers they hear.
   - Go through the answers.

   300 18 1,001 41 115 1,500 700 335 285 60,000
   4,000,000

2   Ask the class to listen again and to repeat each number accurately.
   - Check that students know when to use *and* in large numbers (see **Language notes**).
   - Play the recording again, if necessary.

   Either: before the last two numbers; *or*: if the last number is less than ten, before the last number

Reading

3   Ask students to cover up the leaflet about the Ritz and look instead at the pictures. Get students to describe what they can see and encourage them to share any information they may already know about the hotel.
   - Now get the class to read the questions and guess the correct answers, following the example.

4   Ask the students to read the hotel leaflet to see if their guesses from Exercise 3 were correct. Make sure they don't read the postcard at this stage.

   1 115 rooms   2 £295+   3 £1,650+   4 £370+   5 £44

5   Focus attention on the postcard and elicit who it's from and to. (*It's from a family who stayed at the Ritz,*

to Peter Woodley in New Zealand.) Ask students to read the questions, then to answer them by reading the postcard.

   1 The hotel's got a TV with 30 channels in their room.
   2 They have breakfast in bed; there's an excellent fitness centre, a restaurant and there's a babysitting service.
   3 They are too busy doing things in the hotel.

6   Ask students to look at the postcard again, this time to fill in the gaps with the exact words.
   - Go through the answers. Ask if 's is short for *is* or *has*.

   1 's got (*has got*)   2 have

Grammar focus

7   Ask students to refer to the examples in order to complete the explanations. (See also **Language notes**.)

   1 have/have got   2 have

Practice

8   Ask the class to answer the questions with *have* or *have got*. Make sure students realise two answers are possible for some questions.

   1 A: have / have got; B: has / has got
   2 A: has / has got; B: haven't got / don't have
   3 A: Does have; B: does
   4 have
   5 has / has got
   6 hasn't got / doesn't have
   7 A: has / has got; B: hasn't / hasn't got
   8 has / has got

Get talking

9   Divide the class into two groups (As and Bs). As work together to complete their questions using *have got* or *have*, and Bs do the same with theirs. Check each group has the correct questions.

   Student A:
   Which city has 56 museums / art galleries?
   (Answer: San Francisco)   How many restaurants has the Hard Rock Café got in the world? (Answer: 112)
   Which underground system has 4.3 million passengers a day? (Answer: New York)
   Which restaurant chain has got restaurants in 57 countries? (Answer: Burger King)   Which city has got 274 underground stations? (Answer: London)
   Which restaurant chain has 45,000,000 customers a day? (Answer: McDonald's)

   Student B:
   How many restaurants has Burger King got in the world? (Answer: 11,188)   Which city has 700 live music events every week? (Answer: London)   Which city has 5 airports? (Answer: London)   Which city has 1000 mm of rain per year? (Answer: Mexico City)
   Which restaurant chain has 15,000,000 customers a day? (Answer: Burger King)   How many stations has the New York subway got? (Answer: 468)

   - Ask students to check their answers.
   - When they are ready, ask students to form pairs (A + B) to take it in turns to ask and answer their questionnaires.
   - At the end, ask which piece of information surprised them the most.

Vocabulary	Food and drink
Grammar	*Some, any, much, many, a lot of*
Language to go	Discussing what you eat and drink

Food for thought

Language notes

- Although the meaning of the vocabulary in Exercise 1 will not be a problem, check pronunciation. Point out any 'silent syllables' and be prepared to spend time on drilling, e.g.
  veg(e)tables /ˈvedʒtəbəlz/; *choc(o)late* /ˈtʃɒklət/; *on(i)ons* /ˈʌnjənz/; *bisc(u)its* /ˈbɪskəts/; *strawb(e)rries* /ˈstrɔːbrɪz/; *fru(i)t* /fruːt/.
- The use of *some* and *any* at this level is limited to *some* for positive statements and *any* for questions and negatives. A typical mistake is to use *some* instead of *any*, e.g. ~~We don't have some fruit.~~ [*any*] You may want to tell students that *some* is often used in questions when the expected answer is 'yes', e.g. *Would you like some tea? Can I have some milk?*
- We use *a lot of / (not) much* to talk about a large amount with *uncountable* nouns, e.g. *Drink a lot of water but don't eat much chocolate.* We use *a lot of / (not) many* to talk about large numbers with *countable* nouns, e.g. *I eat a lot of vegetables, but not many cakes.* A typical mistake is to use *much* and *many* in the affirmative, e.g. ~~I eat much fruit and many vegetables.~~ [*a lot of*]

Way in

- Set a time limit of one minute and ask students to brainstorm different kinds of food and drink. At the end of this time, write students' suggestions on the board in two columns – countable and uncountable nouns.
- Ask students to say why you have put them in different columns.

Vocabulary and speaking

1 Ask students to look at the pictures and match them to the words.
   - Do the first one with the class as an example.

1 C	2 A	3 B	4 D	5 I	6 L
7 E	8 J	9 K	10 G	11 F	12 H

2 ▭ Play the recording and get students to listen and repeat the words.
   - Draw attention to the fact that often the pronunciation isn't the same as the spelling. (See 'Language notes' above.)

3 Divide the class into pairs to discuss the two questions. They should, at this stage, only talk about the food and drink from Exercise 1.
   - At the end, ask a few students to report back to the class.

Reading and listening

4 Focus attention on the text and ask students where they might see it. (In a TV/Radio guide.) Ask students to read the text and answer the question.

   a) healthy food

5 Ask a stronger student in the class to say if they think chocolate is good or bad for you, and then to give a reason for their answer. Focus attention on the table and ask students to do the same for the other foods listed.

6 ▭ Now ask the class to listen to the radio programme and write the speaker's opinions, *good* or *bad*, in column 2. Did the speaker agree with them?

7 Play the recording again – this time to find the reasons for the opinions. Ask students to write the reasons they heard in column 3.
   - Students do the activity and check with a partner.
   - Go through the answers.

	2	3
chocolate	good	live longer
salt	good	live longer
bread	good	lose weight
potatoes	good	lose weight
fruit	bad	too much acid
coffee	good	anti-depressant
tea	good	helps you think

Grammar focus

8 Ask students to look at the examples in order to choose the best options to complete the two explanations. (See also Language notes.)

   1 b
   2 b / a

Practice

9 Ask the class to look at the sentences and underline the correct words, following the example.
   - Students check their answers in pairs.

1 A much B a lot of	2 A many B a lot of
3 A much B a lot of	4 A many B many
5 A much B much	

10 Divide students into As and Bs. They take it in turns to ask each other the questions from Exercise 9 (part A of each dialogue). They should answer in a way which is true for them.
   - Do an example with the class by asking a student to ask you an A question and answering in a way that is true for you.

Get talking

11 First, ask students individually to make notes of the food they eat at each meal. Ask them to write how much they eat, and if it is good for them or not.
   - Divide the class into small groups to decide who has the healthiest diet.
   - Get the groups to report back to the class and see who has the healthiest diet in the whole class.

LESSON **15**
Modals

Vocabulary British and American words for clothes
Grammar Present and past obligation with *have / had to*
Language to go Talking about obligation

A nice place to work

Language notes

- *Have (has) to / had to* are used to express obligation and show that something is necessary. Check students realise there's no choice. Negative forms have a different meaning which is sometimes confusing for students. *Don't have to / didn't have to* mean that there is no obligation. It is *not* necessary, and so there is a choice, e.g. *I don't have to wear a suit.* (Check by asking *Is it OK to wear a suit? Yes. / Is it OK not to wear a suit? Yes.*)
- Pronunciation: '*to*' in *have to / had to* is pronounced as a weak form /tə/ when followed by a consonant: *I have to* /həvtə/ *start work at 9 a.m.*

Way in

- Ask the class in which country you would find *hamburgers, baseball* and *the Empire State Building,* to elicit *the USA.* Divide the class into pairs and give them two minutes to think of as many things as possible they associate with the *USA.* Write students' suggestions on the board.

Vocabulary and speaking

1   Remind students that there are some words which are different in British and American English, for example *trainers* and *sneakers.*
    - Ask students to look at the pictures and match each of them to an American AND a British word.
    - Students describe the clothes people are wearing in the photo.

    1-9-E   2-7-A   3-6-C   4-10-D   5-8-B

2   Ask the class to look at the dialogue and tell you what the situation is. (In a clothes shop, A is a customer, B is an assistant.) Tell them some words are in American English, but you would like them to 'translate' them into British English.
    - Do the first sentence together.
    - After feedback, get them to practise saying the dialogue with a partner.

    A: Hi. I'm looking for some trousers to go with my favourite jumper.
    B: How about these? They look great with trainers.
    A: I don't know. I don't often wear trainers.
    B: Or these? They come with a free waistcoat.
    A: Thanks. I'll try them on. And do you have any vests?
    B: Yes, of course. You'll find some over there.

Listening

4   📖 Draw a picture of a stick man in a suit /suːt/ and tie on the board. Ask students to describe what he is wearing. Elicit occupations where people commonly wear a suit (bankers, accountants, lawyers, etc.). Tell them they are going to listen to a man talking about his job, and what he wears for work.
    - Tell students to read the sentences before they listen. Ask for suggestions about what 'dressdown days' could mean. (Days where people who normally have to wear suits, etc. can wear casual clothes to work.)

- Play the recording for students to decide if the sentences are true or false.
- Students check their answers with a partner before listening again.

    1 False   2 False (he wears office casual)   3 True
    4 False   5 True   6 False   7 True (flexi-time)   8 True

Grammar focus

5   Ask students to read the four sentences and then find an example sentence for each explanation. Draw attention to the pronunciation (see **Language notes**) and remind students about the third person – *He has to wear clothes that look good.*

    1 It isn't necessary – *You don't have to wear casual clothes.*
    2 It is necessary – *We have to wear clothes that look good.*
    3 It wasn't necessary – *We didn't have to wear suits on Fridays.*
    4 It was necessary – *We had to wear suits every day.*

Practice

6   Ask students to write sentences using the correct form of *have to,* following the example. Remind them to think about tense.
    - Students do the activity and check their answers with a partner.

    1 *You don't have to* work from 9 a.m. to 5 p.m.
    2 *Did* they *have to* wear formal clothes before 1996?
    3 He *has to* carry a mobile phone at all times.
    4 She *doesn't have to* wear smart clothes.
    5 *Do* you *have to* speak many languages?
    6 We *didn't have to* go to the office every day last year.
    7 They *had to* arrive early yesterday morning.
    8 *Do I have to* have a computer at home?

Get talking ...

7   Ask students to make notes individually about where they work or study. Suggest they look at the ideas in the book to help them.
    - Divide the class into pairs to discuss their ideas.

... and writing

8   Ask the class to write a letter to a friend who is coming to work in their country. Get them to help their friend with information about work practices, e.g. clothes, forms of address, hours of work, length of breaks, meals, smoking policies, etc.
    - Get them to follow the example of how to start the letter and encourage them to read each other's letters at the end.
    - You may wish to use the photocopiable model in the Writing bank (page 147) to focus on the conventions of writing an informal letter.

Vocabulary Topics for TV soaps
Grammar Future predictions with *will* / *won't*
Language to go Predicting the future

Mumbai Soap

Language notes

- The modal verb *will* / *will not* is used to make predictions about the future. These predictions are based on personal opinions and not on factual information.
- Draw attention to the contracted forms of *will* both after a pronoun, e.g. *I'll do it* /aɪldu:wɪt/, and after a word other than a pronoun where it is pronounced as a separate syllable, e.g. *Jim'll do it* /dʒɪməldu:wɪt/. The negative *will not* is usually contracted to *won't* /wəʊnt/, e.g. *He won't forget her*.
- We can also use *I think* + *will* to make predictions based on personal opinions, e.g. *I think he'll marry her. Do you think he'll marry her?* For negatives we usually say, e.g. *I don't think he'll marry her*; not ~~I think he won't marry her.~~

Way in

- Elicit the names of the different kinds of TV programme, e.g. documentary, game show, drama, nature / wildlife programme, cartoon, film, the news, chat show, etc. In pairs, students say which they like watching, and why. You might want to use this opportunity to revise some basic adjectives (*boring, interesting, silly, fun*, etc.).

Reading and speaking

1 If you did the 'Way in' activity and students talked about the topic of soap operas (*soaps*) ask those students to tell the others what soaps are. (See also **Background information** below.)
   - Ask students to discuss the questions in pairs.
   - Find out where the most popular soap operas in the students' own countries come from.
   - Find out if anyone knows any Indian soap operas and give them some background to the Indian film industry.

   Background information
   A *soap opera* or *soap* is a long-running TV drama about the lives of a group of people. *Soaps* are usually shown three or four times a week for about 30 minutes. Favourite soap topics are *love, marriage, crime* and *family life*. The most popular ones in Britain are *EastEnders*, set in London, *Coronation Street*, set in Manchester and *Brookside*, set in Liverpool. For the most popular episodes, about 18 million people watch (nearly a third of the UK population).
   Mumbai, formerly known as Bombay, is the home of the Indian film industry *Bollywood*, named after *Hollywood*. The Indian film industry first started in the early years of the twentieth century. Now, *Bollywood* is a huge industry and Mumbai produces more than half of all Indian films each year. Many of *Bollywood's* films follow a formulaic pattern of a love story, with large numbers of songs and dances as well as choreographed fight scenes. Stars of the films earn a lot of money and are very famous.

2 Tell students they are going to read about a TV drama made in India called *Mumbai Soap*. The main characters are Mina and Sanjay. Ask them to look at the first photograph and predict what Mina's problem could be.

- Students then read part 1 of the story to see if they were correct.

   Mina believes her parents, who she loves and respects, will never accept Sanjay, the man she loves.

3 Check the story so far, then elicit suggestions from students about what they think Mina will do next.
   - Ask students to read the three possibilities and to tell their partner which one they think most likely, and why.

4 Students read part 2 to check their predictions.

   Option c is correct.

5 Repeat the process by asking students what they think will happen next and why.
   - Again, ask them to choose from the next three possibilities, and discuss their choice briefly with a partner.

6 Students now read part 3 to check their predictions.

   Option b is correct.

Listening

7 📖 Finally, ask them to listen to the story so far and predict how it will end. Ask a member from each group to report their ideas to the class. Students give their own answers.

Grammar focus

8 Focus attention on the examples of future predictions and ask students to underline the correct words in the two explanations. You may want to use the students' own predictions from Exercise 7 to highlight the structures.

   1 personal opinion
   2 *don't think* + *will*

9 📖 Play the recording (more than once, if necessary). Ask students to listen and repeat the sentences accurately. (See also '**Language notes**'.)

Practice

10 Explain that they are going to look at a page from a TV guide.
   - Get them to complete the text with *will* or *won't* and a verb from the box. Do the first one on the board as an example.
   - Students do the activity and check with a partner.
   - Go through the answers. Did anyone predict this?

1 will get	2 'll phone	3 won't speak
4 will meet	5 will go	6 'll recognise
7 will be	8 'll have to	

Get talking

11 Explain that there are five situations. The task is to predict what will happen in each situation.
   - Divide the class into small groups and ask students to discuss each situation.
   - Tell them to write down their own personal predictions for each situation.
   - At the end, students can pin their predictions up around the class for others to read. In the next lesson, or the following week, check to see whose predictions were the most accurate.

Vocabulary Adjectives describing places and objects; transport
Grammar Superlatives
Language to go Using superlatives to describe places

Camden Market

Language notes

- Reinforce the concept that superlatives are used to compare three or more things or people, while comparatives are used to compare only two.
- Draw attention to the spelling rule that if a one-syllable adjective ends in a vowel followed by a consonant, we need to double the consonant for both comparatives and superlatives: e.g. *big – bigger – (the) biggest*.

Way in

- Write the word 'market' on the board and ask students to think of different kinds of markets and of things they would normally expect to find there, e.g. *fruit, vegetables, stalls, market traders,* etc. Use this opportunity to pre-teach useful vocabulary.

Vocabulary and speaking

1 Ask the class to look at the photo of Camden Market (but not to read the advert at this stage) and discuss what they can see. *Has anyone been to Camden? Where is it? What do you think it's like?* (See '**Background information**'.)
- Have a brief class discussion about markets.

Background information
Camden Town is in North London. The town's original craft market, called *Camden Lock Market*, was started in 1974. Its name comes from the 'lock', where the river boats pass through the canal beside the market. The busiest times are Saturdays and Sundays, when sometimes there are also street entertainers. People come from all over the world.

2 Ask the students to look at the text and choose the correct adjective. Encourage them to read the text before choosing the correct adjective.
- Students do the activity and check in pairs.
- Go through the answers. Check comprehension of *trendy* – an informal word meaning fashionable, and *ethnic handicrafts* – goods made in countries a long way from the UK or the US, which seem very different and unusual.
- Point out that learning adjectives and their opposites (antonyms) at the same time is a useful aid to memory.

1 trendy	2 attractive	3 busy
4 famous	5 second-hand	

Reading

3 Focus attention on the advert for Camden Market and ask why it was written (*to encourage people to visit Camden*).
- Make sure students read the questions before reading the advert.
NB *by train* usually refers to the overground train system; *by tube* is specifically the London underground train system. In the USA and other English-speaking places, underground train systems are referred to as the *subway* or *metro*.
- Students do the activity and check with a partner.

1 a It has the widest selection of second-hand clothes.
  b It has the capital's most interesting art.
  c It has the trendiest cafés, bars and restaurants.
2 The tube is the quickest way.
3 The bus is the cheapest way.
4 You can also go by train, car or taxi.

Grammar focus

4 Ask the class to look at the examples of superlative forms and to use this information to answer the three questions. (See also '**Language notes**'.)

1 no   2 no   3 no

- Elicit spelling rules for making comparatives and superlatives, and spend time on pronunciation.

Practice

5 Ask students to make questions using the superlative form of the adjectives, following the example.
- Go through the answers.

1 is the cheapest way
2 is the easiest way
3 is the worst thing
4 is the biggest problem
5 is the most interesting
6 is the best thing
7 is the most popular
8 is the busiest time

6 In pairs, get students to ask and answer the questions they made in Exercise 5. Students should answer in ways which are true for them.
- Do an example with the class by asking a student to ask you the first question.
- As students are working, walk round the class and check they are using the new language accurately.

Get talking ...

7 Ask students to choose a tourist destination they know well. If students are from the same area, they could work together.
- Get them to look at the discussion points in their books.
- After working on the points individually, or in pairs, get them to discuss their ideas in groups.
- Have a class vote about which place would be the most interesting to visit.

... and writing

8 Ask students to write an advertisement for the tourist attraction they spoke about in Exercise 7. Encourage students to pin up their adverts so other students can read them.
- You may wish to use the photocopiable model in the Writing bank (page 152) to focus on the conventions of writing advertisements.

LESSON **18**
Present perfect

Vocabulary   Travel: verb + noun combinations
Grammar   Present perfect with *yet* and *already*
Language to go   Saying what you've done so far

On the move

Language notes

- It may be useful for students to know that you can extend the travel verb combinations for use with a variety of different nouns, e.g.:
  to book a ticket, a hotel room, a theatre or cinema ticket, a table in a restaurant.
  to renew a passport, your driving licence, a visa.
  to transfer some money, your job location.
  to pack the cases, the bags, the car.
  to get a visa, some passport photos.
  to rent a flat, a car, a machine.

Way in

- Write the following stem sentence on the board and ask students to complete it in their own words: *I never leave home without* … Students discuss their responses in pairs followed by feedback. Help with vocabulary as necessary (e.g. *keys, wallet, ID card, mobile phone, umbrella*).

Vocabulary and speaking

1   Ask students to look at the picture and use it to teach or elicit the travel vocabulary *suitcase, passport, ticket, money, clothes, camera, book, tennis racket, video, teddy bear*.
- In pairs, ask students to decide which of the items they usually take / never take with them when they travel, and also make a list of anything else they might take.
- Ask a few students to report back to the rest of the class.

2   Ask the class to match the beginnings and the endings of the sentences in the two columns, following the example.

1 b   2 a   3 e   4 f   5 c   6 d

Listening

3   📖 Explain that they are going to listen to a conversation between Mel and her friend. Mel is going to travel soon. Ask students to read the questions first and then listen to find the answers.
- Students underline the correct answers, then check with a partner.

1 a   2 b   3 b

4   Get the class to look at Mel's list of travel preparations. Make sure students understand the instructions and that they are to tick the things on the list she has completed.
- Play the recording again, allowing time for students to check their answers with a partner before playing the recording for a final time.
- Go through the answers.

- sell the car
- have vaccinations
- renew passport
- book the ticket
- book a hotel room

Grammar focus

5   Ask students to refer to the examples to complete the explanations. You may need to spend some time revising how the present perfect is formed. (*have / has* + past participle)

1 already   2 not yet   3 yet

Practice

6   Ask students to look back at Mel's list in Exercise 3 and see what she has, and hasn't done.
- Ask them to make sentences using *already* and *yet*, following the example.

She's already sold the car.
She hasn't transferred her money yet.
She's already had her vaccinations.
She's already renewed her passport.
She hasn't got her visa yet.
She's already booked the ticket.
She's already booked a hotel room.
She hasn't packed her cases yet.

7   Let pairs compare answers and check they are correct.
- Elicit the question form using *yet*, as in the example.
- Practise the example.
- Students ask and answer all the questions – make sure they use the new language accurately.

Get talking

8   Explain that students are going to role-play three colleagues who are going abroad (e.g. on a business trip). Each colleague has a number of things to do to prepare for the trip.
- Divide students into groups of three (A, B, C) and ask Student A to look at list A and so on. Check they understand all the vocabulary in the lists.
- Individually, students should then tick two of the things on their list they have already done.
- When they have done this, they should take it in turns to ask each other questions e.g. *Have you renewed the passports yet?* to find out which tasks have already been done, and which are still to do.
- Finally, ask them to make a list of all the things which still must be done. Get them to decide who is going to do each thing and when.

Vocabulary   Sports: word building
Function   Past ability with *could* and *be good at*
Language to go   Talking about how well you could do things

Real fighters

Language notes

- The word families in Exercise 1 offer students a useful extension of their basic vocabulary. The principle behind this exercise can be extended to many other words. Students may be surprised at how much they already know.
- Two ways of describing ability in the past are covered in the lesson:
  a) the modal verb *could* / *couldn't* + infinitive (without *to*)
  b) *was* / *were good at* (something).
- Adverbs of degree (previously discussed in Lesson 2) allow the speaker to show the strength of adjectives or adverbs:

really	quite	not very	not at all
+ +	+	–	– –

Way in

- You could start the lesson by checking / revising the 'activity' verbs used in the lesson.
- Write some or all of the verbs on slips of paper: *box, fight, swim, cycle, run, dance, ski, play the piano, play golf, take photos, sing, speak a foreign language, cook, drive, read.*
- Show each verb to a different student in turn, who mimes the verb for the class to guess. You could demonstrate one yourself first.

Vocabulary and speaking

1   Focus attention on the table and ask students to fill in the gaps in the table. Encourage them to use monolingual dictionaries if they are to hand.
- Draw attention to the difference between *to fight* (general verb: to use physical violence against someone) and *to box* (more specific verb: to fight someone with fists (closed hands)).

> Person: fighter, runner, dancer
> Sport: swimming, cycling, dancing, skiing
> Verb: to swim, to run, to ski

2   Read the example and check students understand the instructions.
- Get a student to ask you about one of the activities to demonstrate and check they understand the possible responses to the second question: *Very well* / *Quite well* / *Not very well.*
- Monitor the pairs as they are speaking.

Reading

3   Get students to look at the photos of the boxers and ask if they know who they are.
- Get them to discuss the questions in pairs without reference to the text.
- Ask a few students to report their ideas but do not give the correct answers at this stage.

4   Students read the text to check their answers in Exercise 3.
- Go through the answers.

> 1 Muhammad Ali and Laila Ali.
> 2 Father and daughter.
> 3 Muhammad started boxing in 1954 aged 12, Laila in 1999 aged 20.
> 4 Muhammad: he was world champion.

5   Ask the class to complete the three parts of the table about Muhammad Ali using information from the text.
- Students read the text and check their answers with a partner.

> Before his illness he could swim, run, skip, box.
> After his illness he could help other people.
> After his illness he couldn't speak well, move quickly, box.

Language focus

6   Ask the students to look at the examples and match the two halves of the explanations. Draw attention to the different forms and ask if we are talking about *now* or *in the past* (in the past).
- Draw attention to the symbols indicating the adverbs of degree (see also '**Language notes**').

> 1 b
> 2 a

Practice

7   Get students to make complete sentences from the prompts and the adverb suggested by the symbol in brackets.
- Do the first example together to show what you mean. Remind them of the symbols in Exercise 6.
- Students do the activity then check in pairs.
- Go through the answers.

> 1 Martin could swim quite well so he joined a swimming club.
> 2 I was no good at playing the piano when I was young but now I can play quite well.
> 3 They couldn't play golf very well so they decided to have lessons.
> 4 We were good at dancing so we entered the salsa competition.
> 5 My brother was really good at taking photos so he was very sad when I broke his camera.
> 6 She could sing quite well before she got ill.
> 7 He wasn't very good at sport at all so he didn't enjoy games lessons at school.
> 8 I couldn't speak Italian at all when I got my first job in Rome.

Get talking

8   Ask the class to work individually to complete the first column in the survey form. They should think of something else they could do ten years ago which should go at the bottom of the form. Remind them to use the same symbols from Exercise 6 to record how well they could do each thing.
- Students work in pairs to ask each other questions. Go through the example if necessary before starting.
- At the end, ask each student to tell the class something they found out about their partner. Is there anything that everybody in the class could do?

Vocabulary   Adjectives to describe advertised products
Grammar   First conditional (*if* + present simple + *will*)
Language to go   Talking about future possibility

The message behind the ad

Language notes

- This lesson introduces combinations of verbs and nouns which are commonly used in the language of advertising, e.g. *delicious coffee, fresh orange juice, shiny hair*. NB *advertisements* are often referred to as *adverts* or *ads*.
- The first conditional (*if* + present simple, *will* + infinitive (without to)), is used to talk about things that are likely to happen as a result of another action / event. This lesson uses the context of advertisements and the language of persuasion found therein to present and practise the first conditional, e.g. *If you buy this shampoo, your hair will look shiny and healthy.*

Way in

- Take in to the class some striking advertisements from a magazine (or recorded from the TV). Display (or play them) and get the class to guess what products they are advertising. It doesn't matter if some of them are already well-known or if they are not in English.
- Discuss whether the students like the adverts and if they would persuade students to buy the products. Why / why not?

Vocabulary

1 Focus attention on the pictures and check students know what each item is in English.
- Ask students to read the sentences and to underline the best adjective to complete the sentence.
- Students check in pairs but don't give the answers at this stage as students will listen for these in Exercise 2.

2 ▭▭ Play the recording so students can check their answers.

> 1 shiny / healthy-looking   2 safe / soft   3 fresh / healthy
> 4 clean / soft   5 fast / reliable

Speaking and listening

3 Divide the class into groups and ask them to choose one of the products in the pictures. Ask them to think of an advert they have seen (in a magazine or on television) for that kind of product and describe it to each other.

4 ▭▭ Elicit what the main task of an advertising executive might be (to think up new adverts for products). Explain to students that they are going to hear an interview in which an advertising executive is describing some of the products in Exercise 1.
- Ask them to listen and decide which products from Exercise 1 are mentioned.
- Students listen and check with a partner.

> car   suncream   washing powder   coffee   shampoo

5 Ask them to read the questions before listening again for the answers.
- Play the recording (more than once, if necessary) and allow time after each playing for students to compare their answers with a partner.

> 1 young, good-looking men and women
> 2 suncream and washing powder
> 3 yes
> 4 yes (but perhaps not always the products)

Grammar focus

6 Ask students to look at the example sentences using the first conditional and then to complete the three rules by underlining the correct words in each explanation.
- Check students understand that the sentence *If you buy this car, you'll meet a beautiful woman* is typical of the kind of language used in adverts. Although this is probably not true, the speaker wants us to believe it *is* a possible event!
- Check comprehension by rephrasing the questions, e.g. *If I don't use suncream, will my kids get sunburnt? (Yes) What will happen if I use it? (They'll be OK.)*

> 1 future
> 2 present
> 3 can come first or second
> 4 is

7 ▭▭ Ask the class to listen to the examples and repeat each sentence accurately.
- Draw attention to the general principle of rising intonation in the middle of the sentence, indicating that it is unfinished, and falling intonation at the end when it is finished.

Practice

8 Explain (or get a student to tell you) the meaning of *slogans* (short, easily remembered phrases used by advertisers). Tell students they are going to complete the slogans using the correct forms of the verbs in brackets.
- Ask the students to look at the example and work through this together.
- Students do the activity and check with a partner.
- Go through the answers.

> 1 taste / won't want   2 use / 'll (will) look
> 3 'll (will) have / eat   4 goes / 'll (will) repair
> 5 buy / 'll (will) get   6 won't feel / exercise
> 7 'll (will) be / wash

Get talking

9 Ask the class to look at the three adverts and say what products they are advertising: (beer, perfume, juice).
- Divide the class into small groups (group A, group B, etc.) and ask them to discuss the questions in their groups.
- They should then write down the message(s) behind the adverts using the first conditional, e.g. *If you drink (Arrow) beer, you'll look cool and you'll meet lots of women.*
- When everyone has finished, ask students to form new groups, e.g. A + B + C + D to compare their ideas.

LESSON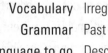
21
The past

Vocabulary   Irregular verbs
Grammar   Past simple and past continuous
Language to go   Describing past events in stories

The story of Grace

Language notes

- The past continuous and the past simple are used for telling stories. The past continuous is often used to set the context of the story. The past simple is used to describe the main action. e.g. *Her father **was out hunting** deer when he **saw** the two young lovers.*
- Note the weak forms of *was* and *were*.
- It may be necessary to remind students that some verbs are not normally used in the continuous tense, e.g. *know, understand, want,* etc.
- You may want to point out the use of *One beautiful summer's day ...*, *One dark night ...* or even *Once upon a time ...* as a device for beginning a story.

Way in

- Think of a big event in everybody's lives. It could be a major news event such as the death of Princess Diana, or a big local event which you know all your students will remember. Ask students to try and remember what they were doing when it happened and write it down. Then ask students to circulate around the class, asking all the other students, e.g.: *What were you doing when Princess Diana died?* Get them to report back to the class, e.g.: *Sara was sleeping when Princess Diana died.*

Listening and reading

1   Students look at picture A and find the words in the box. Students will probably know *river* and be able to guess *country house* from the picture. Don't expect them to know the other words, and don't let them spend too long on this before giving them the correct answers. Check pronunciation.

2   Focus students on the picture at the bottom of the page, and elicit the setting, i.e. it's a police station, and the woman looks shocked / unhappy. Students listen to the first part of the story and answer the questions.

> 1 a police officer   2 She's killed someone.

3   You may want to revise or pre-teach some vocabulary, e.g. *burglar, landowner, shoot / shot.*
- Get students to read individually first. Then ask them to put the pictures in the correct order in pairs. In class feedback, you could check that students fully understand which names refer to which people in the pictures.

> A   C   E   D   B

Grammar focus

4   Ask students to look at the three examples and underline the correct words in the explanations. One example is affirmative, one is negative and one is a question.

> 1 after   2 wasn't

5   Get students to listen and repeat, practising the weak forms of *was* and *were*.
- Write up the words with their phonemic symbols on the board. Check the class understands they are not stressed.

was	were
/wəz/	/wə/

- Stop the recording after each sentence to give students time to repeat and to achieve accuracy.

Practice

6   Get students to complete each sentence using one past simple and one past continuous form. First do the example with the class.

> 1 When Jim Stewart *saw* Sam and Fiona, they *were walking* by the river.
> 2 Fiona *was crying* in her bedroom when Sam *arrived* at the house.
> 3 When Jim Stewart *came out* with a rifle, who *was climbing* the tree?
> 4 Grace *was working* in the garden when Roddy *told* her about her son.
> 5 Where *was* Jim Stewart *sitting* when Grace *gave* him the whisky?
> 6 What *was* Roddy *doing* when she *ran* into the *police* station?

Get talking

7   Divide the class into two groups, As and Bs.
- Ask group A to look at page 84 and discuss the end of the story.
- Ask group B to look at page 87 and do the same.
- Each group should use the combination of questions and sentence beginnings to build up a completed section of the story.
- Re-pair students so that each pair consists of a Student A and a Student B. Each pair then tells each other what they have written, and puts it together to form a completed ending to the story.
- Get pairs to report back to the class on different parts of their endings.

Vocabulary Jobs
Grammar *Like + -ing* and *would like* and infinitive with *to*
Language to go Talking about career preferences

Just the job for you

Language notes

- *Just the job* is an idiom from spoken British English meaning 'exactly what is needed for a particular situation'. *Thanks for lending me your new vacuum cleaner. It was **just the job** for all that dust.* The lesson title therefore carries a double meaning.
- This lesson aims to help students get to grips with the way the verb *like* functions, i.e. *do you like -ing?* and *would you like to* + infinitive? Clearly there is potential for confusion between the two forms and meanings.

Way in

- Ask each student to decide which job they think is more important than any other. Get them to write one sentence to say why.
- Get them to say their choices to the class and write the names of all the job selections on the board.
- Have a quick class vote for each job to see which one they think is most important.
- Get students to consider what this job involves and how well paid it is.

Vocabulary

1 Ask students to look at the pictures. Check pronunciation of the jobs vocabulary.
- Ask them to look at the phrases. If you think any of the phrases will be problematic for your students, you could use the pictures on the page to help clarify meaning. But you probably won't need to teach each phrase like this, as the next step is designed to help show the meanings.
- Students work in pairs and match the jobs with the phrases. Obviously there are more phrases than jobs, so the idea is not simply to find one-for-one matches. Some of the phrases will be clear cut, e.g. *A farmer works outside, A chef works inside*, but equally students may have different opinions about some, e.g. *Does a chef work with people? Does a mechanic work alone?* It's not important to reach a 'right answer' as long as students show that they can use the vocabulary appropriately, and give reasons for their opinions.

Reading and speaking

2 Ask the class to look at the job adverts and match them with the jobs in Exercise 1, following the example. You may wish to use the photocopiable model in the Writing bank (page 152) to focus on the conventions of writing adverts.

1 chef	2 market researcher
3 mechanic	4 barman

3 Now ask them to read the adverts again. Ask them to choose a job they would *like* to do and a job they would *not* like to do. Make it clear that they are imagining about the future, not talking about jobs they do or have done. Ask them to give reasons for their choices.

4 Finally, put the class into pairs to discuss the reasons for their answers in Exercise 3.

Grammar focus

5 Ask the class to look at the examples in the box and decide on the correct verb.

1 would like	2 like

Practice

6 Check that students understand *careers officer* – someone who gives people advice about what the best job would be for them. *Career* is a false friend in some languages – you may want to point out that a *career* is the path you take through your professional life, and not just the time you spend studying at college or university. Explain the situation in the text.
- Tell them that there are a lot of mistakes in the conversation. Show them the example to illustrate what you mean.
- Then ask them to underline and correct all the mistakes.

7 💿 Finally, play the recording to check their answers.

1 like working	2 to earn	3 like
4 likes working	5 he'd like to	6 I like
7 wouldn't want	8 to be	9 visit
10 'd really like		

Get talking …

8 Ask students individually to write down three jobs they would like to do and three jobs they would not like to do. Tell them not to show it to their partners, and keep it for later.
- Students prepare questions about jobs. Show the examples in the book and get them to refer to Exercise 1.
- They interview their partner by asking all the questions they have prepared.
- Ask them to consider the answers to the questions and think of three jobs which their partner would like and three which they would not like.
- Lastly, get them to see if they guessed correctly by checking and comparing their list with the list their partner wrote earlier.

… and writing

9 Get the class to look again at the adverts in Exercise 2. Ask them to write their own adverts for a job they would like to do. Help them as much as possible in class and, if necessary, get them to finish it for homework. You may wish to use the photocopiable model in the Writing bank (page 152) to focus on the conventions of writing adverts.

Vocabulary   Materials and possessions
Grammar   Present simple passive
Language to go Describing the origins of products

Made in the USA

Language notes

- The aim of this lesson is to provide a fairly gentle introduction to the passive, through its use in the present to describe what objects are made of and where they come from.
- We would strongly advise against getting too technical with the grammar, e.g. talking about the agent, etc., but focus instead on 'what is important in the sentence'.
- All the material described, with the exception of *wood*, can be used as both nouns and adjectives, i.e. *silver, leather, cotton, glass, metal, lycra, gold*. The adjective formed from *wood* is *wooden*.

Way in

- Hold up a few items, such as a book, a pen, your wallet, some keys, etc., and elicit the names of the materials they are made from, e.g. paper, plastic, leather, metal, etc.
- Put students in groups and ask them to pool a few of their own possessions. Get them to describe what materials these possessions are made from.

Vocabulary and speaking

1   Ask students to look at the picture of the poster and get them to describe it. The poster is advertising a market called *Fisherman's Wharf* in San Francisco Bay, which is popular with tourists.
- Then ask them to match the objects on the posters with the materials. If they are not clear on the difference between metal and silver, explain that silver is more expensive than metal, and show how it is used for jewellery because of this.

A silver earrings   B glass mirror   C gold rings
D metal candlesticks   E lycra swimming costume
F leather sandals   G cotton T-shirt   H wooden boxes

2   The aim here is for students to practise the vocabulary. Ask them to work in pairs and discuss the questions.
- Ask them to report back to the class and compare their preferences.

Listening

3   📖 Check that students understand the context for the listening. Introduce them to the British tourists, Rachel and Simon, who are shopping at Fisherman's Wharf in San Francisco.
- Then ask them to listen to the recording and find out what Simon buys and why.

glass mirror   because it's cheap

4   Ask the class to listen again and to complete the table with the information they hear about the objects.
- You may wish to pause the recording after each stall, to give students time to think, discuss or write their answers. You may need to play the recording more than once.

object	material	country of origin	price
1 earrings	silver	Mexico	$100
2 boxes	wood	Hungary	$50
3 mirrors	glass	Portugal	$10

Grammar focus

5   Ask the class to look at the examples of the passive and the active forms of the present simple and think about / discuss the questions.
- Then ask them to answer the questions.

1 a   2 a

Practice

6   Help students to decide if the verb is to be in the active or passive form. Then get them to complete the sentences using the verbs in brackets.
- Write the example on the board and check they all understand what to do.
- Ask the class to report back and compare answers.

1 make (*active*)
2 is sold (*passive*)
3 Are these gloves made (*passive*)
4 doesn't buy (*active*)
5 Do they sell (*active*)
6 is bought (*passive*)
7 isn't made (*passive*)
8 are made (*passive*)

Get talking

7   Students turn to pages 84 or 87 and look at the list of objects – encourage them to ask you if they are not sure about any of the vocabulary, e.g. *underwear*, *sweater*.
- Give students time to think about what they are going to say, and make sure they have noticed the example expressions which they can use.
- In pairs, students take turns to describe the objects and their partners have to try and guess what is being described.
- You may want to round off with quick feedback to the class on what was said.

24
Noun phrases

Vocabulary	The theatre
Grammar	*A / an* and *the*
Language to go	Talking about a theatre show

A long run

Language notes

- In this lesson we have chosen to focus on: *a* for the first time we talk about something, *the* when the same thing is mentioned again, *the* when there is only one of something, and *the* with superlative adjectives. You will probably find it unhelpful to give students a complete overview of all the rules about articles, even though they may ask for it!
- We use *an* before a vowel, e.g. *an opera singer*, because of the following vowel **sound** rather than the spelling of the word, so we say *an hour* /ən'auə/ but *a uniform* /ə'juːnɪfɔːm/.
- It is likely that students will make mistakes with articles because of L1 interference. In some languages there are no articles, in others there are articles but they operate in a different way from English.
- The vocabulary work in this lesson deals with commonly confused words related to the theatre.

Way in

- Put students in groups and get them to choose a favourite film or play. Ask them to tell each other what it was and why they liked it.

Vocabulary and speaking

1 Get students to look at the example, then discuss the pairs of words together.
   - Check answers with the class. Check pronunciation, and elicit / explain the difference between the words in each pair.

1 musical	2 play	3 audience	4 composer	5 seats

A theatre is a building.	*A playwright* is a person who writes plays.
An opera is usually more classical and serious in style. Not many words are spoken.	*A musical* is usually less classical, less serious and more modern in style. Many words are spoken.
A play is performed by actors.	*A game:* you can play (v) a game (n) (e.g. football). Actors do not perform games.
Spectators watch events or sport.	*An audience* watches theatrical or musical performances.
A singer sings the music.	*A composer* writes the music.
Seats (not *chairs*) are what you sit on in a theatre.	

2 In pairs, students discuss the questions.
   - Have a quick class feedback.

Reading

3 Explain that they are going to read about two plays.
   - Check that they understand what information to put into the table.
   - Divide the class into two groups (As and Bs). Ask Group A to read about *The Mousetrap* and ask group B to read about *The Phantom of the Opera* on page 87.
   - Ask them to complete the table.

4 Then put one A with one B to pool information and complete the table. Remind them to *talk* about each other's text, not to read what the other has written.
   - Go through the answers together.

The Mousetrap	*The Phantom of the Opera*
1 1952	1986
2 murder mystery	a musical
3 The murderer asks the audience not to tell the secret.	The Phantom helps Christine and Raoul.
4 It has a surprising ending.	The costumes, scenery, the story and the music.

Grammar focus

5 Focus on the examples.
   - Ask the students to complete the explanations.
   - Check the answers with the class.

1 a/an	2 the	3 the	4 the

6 ▭ Play the recording (more than once if necessary) and get students to listen and repeat what they hear. You may need to stop the recording after each sentence to allow time to repeat.
   - Focus on the weak forms /ə/, /ən/ and /ðə/, and the stronger /ðiː/ before a vowel. Ask students to answer questions 1 and 2.

1 /ə/, /ðə/	2 /ən/, /ðiː/

Practice

7 Ask students if they know the story of Romeo and Juliet, and who wrote it (Shakespeare).
   - Get students to complete each gap with *a*, *an* or *the*, following the example.
   - Check the answers with the class, referring back to the rules if necessary.

1 The	2 a	3 a	4 The	5 the	6 a	7 The
8 the	9 a	10 The	11 the	12 the		

Get writing

8 Explain that the students are going to write the story of *West Side Story*. Ask if anyone has seen the film or musical.
   - Reassure them that they do not need to know the story because it is summarised in the exercise. Point out that *West Side Story* is a modern version of *Romeo and Juliet*, so the two stories have similarities.
   - Ask them to look at the outline of the story.
   - Then tell them to write the story using the prompts and using the text in Exercise 7 as a model.
   - Start by putting the students into pairs to write.
   - Walk around and give help if they need it.
   - Start writing in class. If time is short, ask students to finish it for homework.
   - You may wish to use the photocopiable model in the Writing bank (page 150) to focus on the conventions of writing a story.

Vocabulary	Verb + noun combinations
Grammar	*Have to, don't have to, mustn't*
Language to go	Expressing obligation and prohibition

Smart agreements

Language notes

- Guard against the tendency for students to use *must* when *have to* would be more appropriate, as this can sound unintentionally aggressive.
- The distinction between *you mustn't*, which is a prohibition, and *you don't have to*, implying a choice in the matter, is a frequent cause of errors, and is very important to emphasise.
- It's also common for students to use *must* to ask about obligation, but in a neutral question they should use *have to*: *Do we have to finish the writing for homework?* The use of *must* in a question implies disapproval or complaint, and so should be avoided by students in most situations: *Must you whistle like that? Must I finish my homework now?*

Way in

- Ask each student to write down (1) what they think is the most important thing in a successful marriage and (2) what they think married couples argue about most. Get them to compare and discuss their answers in small groups. Is it the same for famous couples?

Vocabulary and speaking

1 Ask students to match the columns to make complete sentences. Get them to find the verb and noun combinations that go together best, following the example. Although a number of the vocabulary items will be new to students, encourage them to use the context to help find the matches.
 - Go through the answers with the class.

 1 f   2 h   3 g   4 c   5 b   6 a   7 e   8 d

2 Ask students to choose three things from Exercise 1. Then, in pairs, get them to tell their partner about them, following the example.
 - Get pairs to report a few examples back to class.

Reading

3 Ask students to look at the photos of famous couples and say who they are and what they have in common.

 Michael Douglas and Catherine Zeta-Jones / Jennifer Aniston and Brad Pitt. They are actors / actresses, they are famous married couples. Both couples made agreements before they got married.

 Ask students if they think married life is easier or more difficult if you are famous, and why, and whether they would like to be married to a famous person and why.
 - Ask students to read the question before reading the article. Make sure you do not explain the meaning of *pre-nuptial* as students have to deduce the meaning from the context.
 - Now get them to read the article quickly to find the meaning of *pre-nuptial agreement*.

 An agreement that both partners sign before they get married.

 - Ask students if they think such agreements are a good idea or not. Encourage them to discuss their reasons.

4 Ask students to read the sentences and decide whether they are true or false. Get them to read the article again and mark the sentences, following the example.
 - Check the answers with the class.

 1 False
 2 False
 3 True
 4 True
 5 True

Grammar focus

5 Ask the class to read the meanings and then match them to the examples. You may wish to highlight the positive, negative and question forms of *have to* on the board, and show how we don't usually use *must* to ask questions about obligation.

 a 2   b 1   c 3

Practice

6 Ask students to complete the activity with the correct forms, following the examples.

1	A: do I have to	B: mustn't
2	A: have to	B: mustn't
3	A: mustn't	B: have to
4	A: do we have to	B: don't have to
5	A: mustn't	B: don't have to
6	A: mustn't	B: don't have to

7 Ask students to read the dialogues in pairs. If you wish, they could swap roles for more oral practice.

Get talking

8 1 Get students, in pairs, to choose one or two situations from the box and discuss in general terms how to make them successful (e.g. if you're going into business with a friend, make sure there is a clear agreement, and that you both know how much money you're putting in and how much you're each going to earn, who is going to do which jobs, etc.).
 2 Ask them to choose one of the situations they discussed and, in the same pairs, draw up a smart agreement.
 - Ask pairs to report back to the class and compare their agreements. See which pair seems to have the best agreement for each situation.
 - You may want to put some of the agreements on the wall for everyone to read.

LESSON **26**
The future

Vocabulary   Food: meat, vegetables, fruit
Grammar   The future with *going to* and *will*
Language to go   Planned and spontaneous decisions

Australian barbecue

Language notes

- As mentioned in Lesson 6, students very often overuse *will*, because they think of *will* as being the only way to express the future.
- Make sure to remind students that the contracted form of *will* is usually used in spoken English, e.g. *I'll cook it for you.*
- You may want to highlight the following pronunciation features when you are discussing food: In *lamb* /læm/ the *b* is not pronounced; *fruit* /fruːt/ is pronounced as one syllable only; *oranges* /ˈɒrɪnʒɪz/ has three syllables with the stress on the first syllable; *onions* is pronounced /ˈʌnjənz/.

Way in

- Ask students to write down their favourite food. In pairs, they then take turns to ask questions to guess what their partner's favourite food is, e.g. *Is it sweet? Is it a vegetable? What colour is it?* You could demonstrate this first with your own favourite food. The 'rules' for this don't have to be very strict, so they could give each other clues, etc. Conduct some brief feedback to the class.

Vocabulary and speaking

1 Ask students to look at the picture. Check pronunciation of the different food items, paying attention to those mentioned in '**Language notes**'.
- Students look at the table in Exercise 1. You may want to do one or two examples with them so that they know what to do.
- Students complete the table.
- When checking students' answers, check understanding by asking concept questions e.g. *Does lamb come from a sheep or a cow? What other colours can a pepper be? (red or yellow).*

meat – beef / pork / lamb / chicken
vegetables – onions / green peppers / mushrooms / carrots
fruit – strawberries / oranges / apples / pineapple

2 'Where you live' in the rubric can be interpreted flexibly, depending on your teaching situation. If all your class are living in their home town, they can talk about eating habits in their own family / home. If you have students of different nationalities, it's an opportunity for cross-cultural comparison of eating habits in different countries.
- Check that students understand *vegetarian*, *barbecue* and *cook*.
- When they have finished talking, get them to report back for a class discussion.

Listening

3 📖 Explain that Lisa and Mike, the Australian couple in the photo, are planning a barbecue.
- Ask students to read the questions and then listen to the recording.
- Students answer the questions; play the recording again if necessary.

1 On the beach
2 Jan and Monica are vegetarians.
3 They are going to cook *vegetable* kebabs for Jan and Monica and meat ones for everyone else.

4 Ask students to look again at the food in the picture. Ask them if they can remember which foods were mentioned in the recording. Don't check or correct answers here, as they are going to listen again to check.
- Students listen to the recording again. Ask them to tick the foods they hear.
- Check the answers together with the class. By elimination, they should be able to say which foods are not mentioned.

They don't mention pork, strawberries or carrots.

Grammar focus

5 Ask students to underline the correct words in the explanations. You may want to draw a simple timeline on the board to show, for each structure, when the decision was made in relation to when the speaker explains their decision about the future.

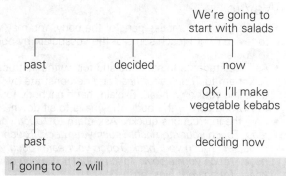

1 going to   2 will

Practice

6 Make it clear to the students that the sentences and their continuations are in pairs, so they have to match parts (a) and (b) within each pair.
- Go through the example with students, and check they understand that in 1, the speaker is deciding now, whereas in 2 the decision has already been taken before the moment of speaking.
- Students match the sentence parts.
- Go through the answers with the class.

1 b   2 a   3 a   4 b   5 b   6 a   7 a   8 b

Get talking

7 Ask the class to imagine that they want to invite a British family to eat with them. With the whole class, discuss what the family may want to eat.
1 Then put the class into small groups. Ask them to discuss when to have the meal, where to have it and what food and drink to have.
2 Get them to make a list of things to eat and drink and ask members of each group to offer to make or bring the different food and drink, following the guidance given. At this stage they should be using *will*, as they are deciding at the moment of speaking.
3 Finally ask each group to report back to the class, using *going to* as they are explaining what they have already decided. Students could vote on the best meal.

Vocabulary Medical symptoms; the body
Grammar Adjectives ending in -ed and -ing
Language to go Describing how you feel

Irritating illnesses

Language notes

- It is very common for students to confuse the use of adjectives ending in -ed (how you feel) with those ending in -ing (what or who makes you feel that way), e.g. *I was frightened because the film was frightening. This book is interesting; I'm interested in it. I'm annoyed with my brother; he is annoying.*
- Don't get bogged down trying to explain why we say, for example, *backache* but not *throatache*. The best way for students to learn the different ailments is as lexical items in groups, i.e. which ones are *sore*, which ones go with *ache*, etc.
- In any class, discussion of illnesses and allergies requires sensitive treatment. While you may feel that personalisation could be a fruitful avenue, there may be students in the class who do not want to discuss their ailments, particularly allergies causing embarrassing rashes, for example.

Way in

- Play a game to practise parts of the body. You may want to revise or pre-teach some of the vocabulary by pointing to yourself.
- Ask the students to stand up and follow the instructions. Ask them to *Touch your head* and demonstrate by touching your own head. Explain that if anybody touches the wrong part of the body, they have to sit down.
- Give the instructions quickly. Ask them to *Touch your legs. Touch your stomach. Touch your neck. Touch your shoulder. Touch your back. Touch your ear. Touch your nose. Touch your elbow. Touch your lip. Touch your knee. Touch your hips,* etc.
- Continue the game until there is only one student standing. This is the winner.

Vocabulary and speaking

1 Ask students to look at the picture. Elicit that the people are all ill, checking that they understand the adjective *ill* and the related adjective *illness* in the lesson title. Elicit that they are at the doctor's.
- Ask them to read the list of symptoms. Elicit that a *symptom* is a sign of illness.
- Get them to match the people to the symptoms.

2 🔊 Ask them to listen to the recording to check their answers. Pause the tape to give them time to check. Explain that the woman in E is coughing / has a cough, and other symptoms such as a headache, which altogether make a cold.

a headache D	a sore throat C	a rash B	a cold E
a backache G	a stomachache A	an earache F	

- Play the recording again, stopping after each word to give students time to repeat.

3 Check that students understand *heavy, hat, scarf, honey, lemon, vitamin C, scratch.* Ask them to read through the list of advice and make a note of which symptom each one might go with.
- Role-play an example dialogue with the class using the model given.
- Students practise the dialogue in pairs, taking it in turns to begin. Get them to work through the list, reminding them to start each dialogue with *What's the matter?*

Reading

4 Elicit from students that the text is from a medical problem page in a magazine by referring to the headings in the magazine feature.
- Ask them to read the questions first and check they understand the vocabulary. Check *depressed, annoyed, worried.*
- Ask students to read the text to find the answers as quickly as possible.
- Go through the answers together.

1 Alex: sore throat	3 Alex D
Sarah: headache	Sarah E
Frances: a rash	Frances A
2 Frances is worried.	
Sarah is depressed.	
Alex is annoyed.	

5 Ask students to read the text again and match the problems with the answers. You may need to explain the meaning of *allergic.*

1 b	2 c	3 a

Grammar focus

6 Focus on the box and ask students to look at the examples.
- Then ask them to underline the correct words in the explanations. You could write more examples on the board (See 'Language notes'.)

1 -ed	2 -ing

Practice

7 First do the example with the class.
- Then let students work individually and then compare answers with a partner.
- Go through the answers with the class.

1 A: worrying	1 B: worried
2 A: interesting	2 B: interested
3 A: shocked	3 B: shocking
4 A: frightened	4 B: frightened

8 Students work in pairs to practise the dialogues.

Get talking

9 Divide students into As and Bs.
- Explain that the As are patients. Get them to read page 84 and make notes individually on their symptoms and how they feel.
- Tell the Bs that they are doctors. They should look at page 87 and make notes individually on how to give advice.
- In their pairs, students role-play the conversation. Students could reverse roles if there is time.
- Listen to their conversations and note any errors using the adjectives for feedback afterwards.

Vocabulary   Furniture and fittings
Grammar   Present perfect to describe present result
Language to go   Talking about changes you can see

Changing rooms

Language notes

- This unit focuses on one use of the present perfect, 'present result'. It exemplifies the present perfect as a 'bridge' tense, linking a past action with a present result.
- Note the pronunciation of *cupboard*, where the *p* is not pronounced. [ˈkʌbəd]

Way in

- Ask the class which is their favourite room in their house. Tell them about your favourite room and give your reasons, e.g. colours, view, furniture, size, atmosphere, etc.
- Put the class into groups to discuss their favourite room. Which room sounds the best?

Vocabulary

1   Students look at the photos. Ask them which rooms they are (kitchen and living room).
- Students work in pairs and match the words with the furniture and fittings in the photos.
- Check answers, focusing on pronunciation of the words.

1 L	2 F	3 K	4 J	5 B	6 A	7 M	8 E
9 G	10 D	11 I	12 C				

2   The aim of this exercise is to teach the verbs used to describe changes to a house: *re-cover, change, polish, remove, paint*.
- Do the example with the class first, and focus on the verb *paint*. Explain that there are new verbs here, so students may find it difficult.
- Students work in pairs to match the sentences with the responses.
- Check answers, focusing on meaning and pronunciation of the verbs, and the nouns with which they collocate.

1 e	2 a	3 d	4 c	5 b

Reading and listening

3   Explain that four people are taking part in a TV programme.
- Students look at the questions, then read the text and answer the questions.
- Check answers together.
- Ask students if they would like to take part in such a programme, and why. Do they have a similar programme in their own country?

1 neighbours	2 change a room in each other's home
3 2 days	4 £500

Background information

Changing Rooms is a popular TV programme in many countries. Two couples who are neighbours exchange houses for two days. They choose one room in their neighbours' house and change the style and furniture completely. Cameras follow the process and a team of experts help. After two days, each couple returns to their house to see their newly decorated room. They usually like it, but occasionally they hate it.

4   ▭ Tell the students that they are going to hear one couple's reaction to the new room.
- Ask them to read the answers before listening.
- Check the answers with the class.

1 generally positive	2 Jason

5   Now ask them to listen again and match the columns to describe what has been done to the room.
- After listening, let them check answers with a partner.
- Finally, go through the answers with the class.

1 e	2 c	3 d	4 a	5 b	6 f

Grammar focus

6   Focus on the examples of the present perfect and the two columns, one for *present result* and one for *past action*. Students read the two explanations and underline the correct words to complete them.

1 past	2 can

Practice

7   Ask students to look at the photo of Megan's and Peter's new kitchen.
- Make sure students understand this is the 'new' version of the kitchen on page 58. In pairs, students use the words in the box to describe the six changes, following the example.

They've put the washing machine in a cupboard.
They've put cupboards on the walls.
They've moved the sink to the other side of the washing machine.
They've put tiles on the floor.
They've put the cooker opposite the sink.
They've put a radiator in.

Get talking ...

8   Explain that they are going to see pictures of a room before and after seven changes have been made to it.
- Student A turns to page 84 and sees the room 'before', and B to page 88 and sees the room 'after'.
- Following the example given, students take turns to describe one aspect of their picture. If they find a difference, they make a sentence in the present perfect about the change that has been made.
- Do a quick class feedback.

painted walls (example); polished floorboards; removed fireplace; moved wardrobe; re-covered armchairs; put up a picture; made/put up new curtains

... and writing

9   Ask students to think about their home or their life in general. What has changed recently? What has been the result of these changes?
- Students write a paragraph describing these changes and results. This could be finished for homework.
- You may wish to have the photocopiable model in the Writing bank (page 147) to focus on the conventions of writing an informal letter.

Vocabulary Table manners
Function Permission
Language to go Asking for, giving and refusing permission

How rude!

Language notes

- It is important to stress that *Is it OK if ... ?* is informal, but it is not necessary to analyse subtle differences between *May I ... Could I ... ?* and *Can I ... ?*
- Polite intonation is important when asking for permission, but don't demand perfect reproduction of the models in the recording. A realistic aim is for students to be aware of the need for polite intonation, and able to produce utterances that sound polite.

Way in

- Ask students in groups to discuss when they have experienced 'rude' behaviour in public. Give an example, e.g. if queuing is a custom locally, describe when someone pushed in front of you.
- Conduct class feedback, comparing a few experiences.

Vocabulary

1   Students look at the picture. Ask where it is (a restaurant) and whether they think people are generally being polite or rude. (rude!)
- In pairs, students answer the questions. The aim is to teach the 'table manners' vocabulary, so tell students not to worry if they aren't sure.
- Check answers with the class, demonstrating actions where necessary. Check pronunciation.

1 B   2 E   3 A   4 F   5 D

Reading and speaking

2   Students look at the statements in quotes. They are examples of behaviour which may be considered rude or not, depending on context and culture. Get students to read a sentence and ask for reactions. Do they agree or disagree?
- Now ask students to read all the sentences in quotes. Explain that first they have to decide whether the statements are true or false for people in their own country.
- Then see if they can decide which are true or false for people living in the UK.
- Put them into pairs to decide on their answers.
- Ask them to report back to the class for feedback.

For the UK
  1 False (It is OK to kiss in public at any time in the UK.)
  2 True
  3 True
  4 False (In formal situations you should let your host pay, but even when invited, people offer to pay for a meal, not expecting the offer to be taken up.)
  5 True (but it's OK to arrive up to about 15 minutes late).
  6 False (You should ask for permission.)
  7 True
  8 False
  9 False (You usually take a bottle of wine in the UK.)
  10 False (A handshake is more usual on a first meeting although it is changing with young people.)

Listening

3   ▭ Explain that students are going to listen to four conversations in different situations. They should listen and match the conversations with the situations. Pause between each conversation to give students enough time to find the situation on pages 60 and 61.

A 6   B 7   C 3   D 4

Language focus

4   Students look at the three columns. Explain that these are all *polite* forms. Get them to read the three headings and match each heading with the correct column.

a asking for permission   b giving permission
c refusing permission

5   ▭ Ask students to listen to the conversations and decide which version is more polite, *a* or *b*. Play the first one to show what you mean.
- You may need to pause the recording to allow them time to decide.

1 b   2 a   3 b   4 b

Practice

6   ▭ Students listen and repeat.
- Pause the recording after each conversation to give students time to repeat.

7   Go through the example with students.
- Get them to try to make the sentences individually and check in pairs.
- Check answers with the class.

(Responses may vary.)
1 May I give you some advice?   Yes, certainly.
2 Is it OK if I take this chair?   I'm sorry but it's taken.
3 Can I have an apple, please?   Yes, sure.
4 Is it OK if I smoke?   I'm sorry, but it's a no-smoking area.
5 Could I borrow your book, please?   I'm sorry. I need it myself.
6 May I leave my bag here, please?   Yes, of course.

8   Students practise the dialogues. Get them to follow the example and use the sentences in Exercise 7.
- Do the first example with the class and then ask students to work in pairs.

Get talking ...

9   Put students in pairs and divide them into A and B. Students turn to their respective page.
- Check they understand that they are asking the person underlined in each situation, and so should choose language appropriate to the relationship.
- Students take turns to read each situation, make a request, and respond as they wish.
- Ask one or two pairs to act out one of their conversations for the class.

... and writing

10 Each student writes two requests: one to you, and one to their partner. Remind them to be polite.
- Let them exchange papers and write a polite response in reply.
- Collect the papers written for you and check them, either while students are writing responses, or later.
- You may wish to use the photocopiable models in the Writing bank (page 151) to focus on the conventions of writing short notes.

Vocabulary Verbs and their opposites
Grammar *Would* + infinitive (without *to*)
Language to go Talking about imaginary situations

What would you do for love?

Language notes

- The aim of this lesson is to provide a gentle introduction to the use of *would* for imaginary situations, without the added complexity of an *if* clause, which is covered in Lesson 40. You may find students want to use *if*; try not to draw too much attention to this, or to correct mistakes with *if* + past, as this will complicate the lesson and possibly confuse students.
- Because *would* is often contracted to *'d* when we speak, e.g. *I'd get some help*, it can be difficult for students to hear, and can lead them to say *I get some help* instead.
- The reading text about obsessive love and jealousy is intended to be fairly light-hearted; try to avoid a heavy discussion at this stage!

Way in

- As a competition, ask students in pairs to think of verbs which are 'opposites' in English (e.g. *come, go*). Give them a time limit of one minute, then check answers and see which pair has the most correct pairs of 'opposite' verbs.

Vocabulary

1 Explain that all the sentences contain pairs of verbs which are opposite in meaning.
   - Show them the example and point out that the opposite of *remember* is *forget*.
   - Get them to follow the example and ask them to underline the correct verb in each sentence.
   - Check the answers with the class. Check understanding where necessary, e.g. *He refused – did he say 'yes' or 'no'?*

1 married   2 sell   3 agreed   4 lose   5 lie   6 move

Reading

2 Ask students to look at the three pictures and describe them briefly. Encourage them to guess what the stories behind them might be.
   - Get them to read the three stories very quickly to see which story matches which picture.

Dangerous pedestrian: C
True love or true madness?: A
Jealous wife: B

3 Ask students to read the sentences and to think about whether they are true or false. Get them to read the three stories again and the comments underneath. Then get them to mark the sentences true or false, following the example.

1 True   2 False   3 False   4 False   5 False
6 True   7 True

Grammar focus

4 Ask students to look at the examples and choose the correct option to complete the explanations.

b

5 [cassette] Ask the class to listen to the recording and repeat. Stop the recording after each sentence to give students time to repeat. Encourage students to use the contracted forms.

Practice

6 Explain to students that you are going to talk about imaginary situations. Ask them to complete the dialogues with *would* or *wouldn't*.
   - Do the first one as an example with the class.
   - Go through their answers together at the end.

1 A: would / sell	B: 'd / sell / wouldn't sell
2 A: would / buy	B: wouldn't / would buy
3 A: would / move	B: 'd stay
4 A: would / marry	B: wouldn't

7 Put students into pairs and ask them to practise the dialogues using their own personal reactions. You may want to do an example with the class by asking a student to ask you a question from part A of the dialogue and giving your own answer to part B. Help students to do the same with the other four dialogues. Make sure they only read from part A and answer with their own response, using part B as a model only. Walk around as they are speaking and help, especially with pronunciation of contracted forms.

Get talking

8 Explain that students are going to write a short questionnaire. Label each pair of students A or B. Pairs turn to their respective pages.
   - Go through the example with the class (the example is exactly the same on both pages 85 and 89). Check that everyone understands there are three alternatives. Then tell all the students to look at their situations and write three possible alternatives for each situation.
   - Monitor pairs closely at first to make sure they know what to do, and to help with ideas if anyone is stuck.
   - When they have finished, students can form either into groups – AABB – or pairs – AB. They then take turns to ask each other their questions.
   - Conduct a brief class feedback, asking a few students to report back their most interesting answers.

LESSON **31**
The past

Vocabulary Crime: word building
Grammar Past simple passive
Language to go Describing a crime

The art of crime

Language notes

• As mentioned in Lesson 23, the passive is generally used when we are more interested in the action than the person or thing that did the action:
e.g. *The Mona Lisa was returned to the museum.*
Sometimes we do not know who or what did the action:
e.g. *Six copies were made.*

Way in

• Write on the board:
Which is worse: stealing a TV from a house; money from a bank; money from someone in the street; food from a shop; a painting from a museum?
• Students discuss the question in pairs, giving reasons for their answers.
• Have a brief feedback discussion with the class.

Vocabulary and speaking

1 Look at the example with students, then ask them to look at the meanings in the right-hand column.
   • In pairs, students fill in any words they know.
   • You may want to allow students to use dictionaries.
   • Conduct feedback, checking understanding. In particular, check:

   Rob a person or place.
   Steal something from someone.

Crime	Criminal	Verb
1 robbery	robber	to rob
2 murder	murderer	to murder
3 burglary	burglar	to burgle
4 mugging	mugger	to mug
5 shoplifting	shoplifter	to shoplift
6 car theft	car thief	to steal a car

2 The aim of 2 and 3 is to practise some of the new crime vocabulary.
   • Students put the crimes in order of seriousness, in their own opinion.
   • Students discuss their opinions in pairs. They don't have to agree!
   • Get a few pairs to report back to the class, giving reasons for their opinions.

3 Use the pictures at the bottom of the page to check that students understand *prison*, *fine*, *execution*.
   • Students discuss the crimes and punishments.
   • Have a brief class feedback.

Listening

4 Students look at the painting. Elicit what it is called.
   • Students try to answer questions in pairs.
   • Check answers with the class.

   1 In Italian it is known as *La Gioconda*.
   2 Leonardo da Vinci.
   3 Louvre Museum, Paris.

5 ▭ Check that students understand the task, and tell them how the names are pronounced in the recording, so that they will recognise them when they hear them.
   • Students listen and match the questions and answers.

• Check answers with the class.

1 a	2 c	3 b

6 Students listen again and decide if the statements are true or false.
   • Do the example together before they start.
   • Play the recording more than once if necessary.
   • Students compare answers before class feedback.

1 False	2 True	3 True	4 False

Grammar focus

7 Ask students to look at the examples and underline the correct word in the explanation. You may wish to highlight the form and use on the board for students.

   passive

Practice

8 Go through the example with students, checking that they understand why the passive is correct here.
   • Students underline the correct form of the verb.
   • Check answers with the class.

1 robbed	2 was burgled	3 arrested	4 murdered
5 was stolen	6 executed	7 was murdered	
8 found	9 took	10 was paid	

Get talking

9 Tell the class that they are going to read and talk about a famous crime that happened in the UK.
   • Put students into pairs and name the pairs A and B alternately round the class. Ask students to turn to their respective pages.
   • Explain that they have a text about a crime, with some blank spaces in it, and that they will have to ask another pair questions to find out the missing information. Ask them to read their first sentence and example question.
   • Then ask students to read the whole text, and each time they come to a numbered space, write a question. Monitor to make sure that everyone knows what to do, and to help with question formation. You may have to prompt students with the question words if they get stuck.

   Student A
   2 Where was the train stopped?
   3 How far was the train driven?
   4 What was shared between the train robbers?
   5 Where were the criminals sent?

   Student B
   2 Who was attacked?
   3 How many bags of banknotes were taken to a farm?
   4 Who was arrested?

   • Students turn to the person the other side of them, so that they are in AB pairs. Student A should ask the first question, then it's important that they take turns to ask each other questions and complete their texts.
   • Check the answers with the class.

Student A	Student B
1 £2 million	1 The Great Train Robbery
2 London	2 The driver
3 One kilometre	3 120
4 The money	4 Most of the criminals
5 To prison	

Vocabulary Phrasal verbs
Grammar Verbs with -*ing* form / infinitive (with *to*)
Language to go Talking about changing habits

Willpower

Language notes

- Phrasal verbs are introduced here as vocabulary items in context. The meanings should therefore be clear and there is no need to go into the grammatical rules behind them at this stage. Encourage students to treat them as individual vocabulary items.
- It's useful for students to recognise verb patterns, and to make a note of these patterns alongside new verbs in their vocabulary books, with an example: e.g.
  to give up (+ verb + -*ing*) – phrasal verb
  Meaning: to stop <u>doing</u> something
  e.g. *He gave up smo<u>king</u> because of his health.*

Way in

Write *start* and *stop* on the board as two headings.
- Elicit and write up things that we start and stop doing, to make our lives better in some way. Give one or two examples. e.g. *start: doing exercise, studying something; stop: smoking, eating chocolate.*
- In pairs, students ask each other what they have started or stopped doing in their life.
- Conduct a brief class feedback.

Reading

1   Focus students on the lesson title, *willpower* (the ability to control your mind and body, so that you can do something difficult). Give an example, e.g. *You need willpower to stop smoking.* Ask a question to check, e.g. *Do you need willpower to do exercise every day?* (yes!)
- Get the class to do the questionnaire to find out how much willpower they have. They should read each question and choose an answer, then check the key on page 86 to see how much willpower they have.
- Let the class compare their answers in pairs then check how much willpower they have.

Vocabulary

2   Now ask them to look at the text again and to find the phrasal verbs. Tell them there are five phrasal verbs. Explain that the phrasal verbs here have two parts. Show them the example before they start.
- Encourage students to use the context to deduce the meaning of the verbs.

| 1 carry on |
| 2 give up |
| 3 cut down |
| 4 throw away |

- Finish with class feedback.

Phrasal verbs	Meanings
throw away	put (something) in the rubbish bin
give up	stop (doing something you've been doing as a habit)
cut down	do less (of something you've been doing as a habit)
take up	begin (generally a hobby, or something you do regularly)
carry on	continue (doing something)

Grammar focus

3   Ask the students to look at the examples in the box. They are all from the questionnaire. Then they look at the other verbs given and decide whether they are followed by an -*ing* form or an infinitive with *to*.

> – *ing* form: likes and dislikes e.g. enjoy.
> – *ing* form: phrasal verbs e.g. give up, take up, cut down on.
> infinitive with <u>to</u>: some other verbs e.g. decide, want, need, learn, provide.

Practice

4   Ask students to complete the paragraph with the correct form of the verbs in brackets.

| 1 to have | 2 going | 3 having | 4 listening |
| 5 to carry | 6 to throw away | 7 to speak | |

Get talking

5   Get students to play the Willpower Game. Use the game board in their book and follow the instructions given.
- Use a coin to show the meaning of *to throw a coin*, *heads* and *tails*.
- Divide the class into groups of 3 or 4. Check all students have a coin.
- Explain that the aims of the game are to speak about the subject on the square in correct English and to be the first to reach the end.
- Demonstrate how to play by doing an example yourself.
- Then play the game. You will have to be the judge of any language disagreements.

Vocabulary   Regular activities: verb + noun combinations
Grammar   Subject and non-subject questions in the present simple
Language to go   Asking questions

A typical day

Language notes

- It's important for students to focus on the difference between subject and non-subject questions, but equally important not to get too bogged down in the grammar; many students seem to pick up the different forms quite intuitively, and too much analysis can dent confidence and do more harm than good! Typical mistakes: ~~Who does pay you?~~ (Who pays you?); ~~How much you get?~~ (How much do you get?).
- For clarity, we have only focused here on question forms in the present, but of course the same rules apply to questions with the past simple.
- There are many nouns which can be combined with *spend*, *do* and *make*. It is best to concentrate for now on the ones introduced in this lesson. These are *pay a bill, empty the rubbish, employ people, spend time, make a phone call* and *do the cooking*.

Way in

- Write or say: *why what when where how*. Don't write (or say) *who*.
- Tell students to write a question starting with *one* of these question words.
- If possible, ask students to walk around the room and ask their question to other students.
- Do a quick class feedback: what was the most interesting question and what was the most interesting answer?

Vocabulary

1   Ask students to look at both columns and match the verbs and nouns that go together.

> 1 d   2 c   3 e   4 b   5 a

2   Now ask them to complete the sentences with verbs from Exercise 1 in the correct form.

> 1 pay
> 2 emptied
> 3 spent
> 4 employed
> 5 make

Listening

3   📼 Ask students to describe the picture. Elicit that it is a party. Tell them there is someone in the picture called Ron, who is there because of *his job*. Students may immediately say it must be one of the waiters or the barman. Don't say whether they are right or wrong at this stage!
   - Students listen to the recording, and decide who Ron is in the picture and what his job is.

> The man on the right with the flowers / He's a *'kissogram'*.

   - You may want to have a brief class discussion about Ron's job. What do students think of it? How would they feel if someone gave them a kissogram?

4   Ask students to listen again and answer the questions.

> 1 He kisses the woman, dances with her, gets everyone to sing Happy Birthday, gives her the cards, reads the message then gives her the flowers.
> 2 She arranges everything, buys flowers, writes messages in the cards.
> 3 Mary, his wife.
> 4 No.

5   Put the students in small groups and get them to choose one of the two topics.
   - Go around the class listening and get students to report one example of each topic back to the class.

Grammar focus

6   Students look at the examples and complete the explanations.

> 1 subject   2 object   3 subject

Practice

7   Ask students to complete the questions using the prompts in brackets.

8   📼 Students listen to the recording and check their answers to Exercise 7.
   - Stop the recording after each sentence to give students time to check.
   - You may want to ask them to repeat the questions.

> 1 Who gets up first in your house?
>   And what time do you get up?
> 2 Do you have a computer at home?
>   Who uses it the most?
> 3 Who makes the most phone calls?
>   Who do you phone the most?
> 4 Who pays the bills in your house?
> 5 Who usually does the cooking?
>   And who empties the rubbish?
> 6 Who do you spend more time with … ?
>   How many evenings a week do you stay at home?
>   Who spends the most time in the house?

Get talking

9   Tell students that they are going to talk about what they do at home.
   - Divide the class into pairs.
   - Then ask them to ask their partners the questions from Exercise 7, about their own lives and their families.
   - Get partners to reverse roles and ask and answer the questions again. Ask them to decide whether their lives are similar or different.
   - Finish with a class feedback.

Vocabulary   Technical equipment
Grammar   Relative clauses with *which*, *that*, *who* and *where*
Language to go   Describing people, places and things

How things work

Language notes

- The rules about choice of relative pronouns are fairly straightforward, but it's common for students to choose the wrong pronoun: *He's the man ~~which~~ I met* [*who*]; *It's a machine ~~who~~ makes copies* [*which*]. This is probably caused by interference from the student's own language, where there is only one relative pronoun for both people and things (e.g. Spanish *que*).
- When the relative pronoun refers to the object of the clause, it is possible to omit it, e.g. *He's the man (who) I met.* For this lesson, it is best to concentrate on practising their inclusion, but be ready for questions about this from the students.
- It isn't possible or necessary to explain the true technical meaning of the word 'digital' as it is used in the context of this lesson. It's sufficient to present it as in the text, i.e. a type of TV which is different from, and better than, 'traditional' TV. Many students will be familiar with the concept of digital mobile phones and digital music recordings, and will understand the word to imply 'better quality'.
- NB *a mobile phone* or *a mobile* (GB). *A cell phone* or *a cellular phone* (US).

Way in

- Ask students to write down the three most important electrical objects they have. Give them an example of your three most important, e.g. *phone*, *radio*, *computer*.
- Pairs tell each other what their three objects are, and why.
- Have a brief class feedback – how many people chose the same objects? Is there one clear 'winner' which is important for most students?

Vocabulary and speaking

1   Students read the four questions and choose answers from the list. Tell them not to worry if they don't know all the words, but to use the pictures on the left to help.

2   📼 Students listen to the recording to check their answers.
- You may need to stop the recording after each sentence to give students time to check.
- Make sure students have clearly understood the meaning of each word.

> 1 A printer and a photocopier can put pictures or text on paper.
> 2 A scanner and a digital camera can make pictures you can look at on a computer.
> 3 A digital TV has a screen and a remote control.
> 4 A mobile phone can go in your pocket and rings when someone wants to speak to you.

3   📼 Ask students to listen and repeat. Stop the recording after each word to give students time to repeat.

> screen   keyboard   remote control
> computer   printer   laptop
> scanner   digital camera   mobile phone
> photocopier   digital TV ['*tee vee*']

4   The aim here is to practise the vocabulary from Exercise 1.
- Ask them to look at the three questions and discuss the answers about themselves in groups.
- Get groups to report back to the class and compare answers.

Reading

5   Ask students to read the five sentences and see if anyone can predict whether they are true or false.
- Get them to read the text and mark the sentences true or false.
- Let them compare answers with a partner before class feedback.
- You may wish to use the picture on page 71 to help explain how we can do many different things with a digital TV that we can't do with traditional TV, and that digital TV allows for two-way communication.

> 1 False   2 True   3 False   4 True   5 False

Grammar focus

6   Ask students to fill the gaps with the pronouns *who*, *which*, *that*, *where* in order to complete the explanations.

> 1 where   2 which or that   3 who or that

Practice

7   Show students how to do this exercise by doing the example with them first.
- Ask them to do the same with all eight sentences, completing them with a clause from the list on the right and *who*, *which*, *that* or *where*.
- Let them check answers in pairs before class feedback.

> 1 c who / that   2 g where   3 f which / that
> 4 a who / that   5 d which / that   6 h where
> 7 e which / that   8 b who / that

Get writing and talking

8   Get the class to play the definitions game, following the instructions and example in their book.
- Give them a couple of examples first by writing a definition on the board and getting them to guess the answer: e.g. *A machine which you take photos with is a camera.*
- Ask students to write six examples individually. Walk around and check they are writing correct sentences. Correct any errors.
- Then put them into small groups to play the game. They read the questions in turn, and the others try to guess the answers. One point for every correct answer.
- Finish with a quick class feedback.

Vocabulary   Sounds people make
Grammar   Present deduction with *must be, might be, can't be*
Language to go   Making deductions

What's that noise?

Language notes

- To keep the concepts clear, we have only presented three modals in the lesson. Students may want to use *could* and *may*. While it is also possible to use these for deductions, we feel it's better to concentrate on fewer forms at first.
- As *must* and *can't* are effectively 'opposites' when used for making deductions, we can't say, e.g. ~~She can be a doctor~~ [*She must be a doctor*] or ~~He mustn't be a pilot~~, [*He can't be a pilot*] both common student errors.
- All the verbs in Exercise 1 can act as nouns in exactly the same form.

VERB	NOUN
to shout	*a shout*
to yawn	*a yawn*
to scream	*a scream*
to whistle	*a whistle*
to cheer	*a cheer*
to clap	*a clap*
to laugh	*a laugh*
to cry	*a cry*

- *A scream* is louder and shriller than *a shout*. When we enjoy something we *cheer* with our voices and *clap* with our hands. *A cheer* is a response to something good; *a scream* may be a response to something bad.

Way in

- Ask students to sit silently for a minute and to make a note of all the noises they hear. See who identified the most sounds.
- You could continue by asking students, for example, to think of all the sounds they can hear in the morning at home before getting up, or at other specific times of the day.

Vocabulary and speaking

1   Ask students to look at the pictures and listen to the recording, to match the sounds with the people in the pictures.
- Play the recording and stop after the first sound to elicit the example answer.
- Then play the rest of the recording as often as necessary, pausing for students to note their answers.
- Ask for class feedback to check their answers.

1 H   2 F   3 C   4 B   5 A   6 G   7 E   8 D

2   Now ask the class to match the people in the pictures with the eight verbs.
- Do an example first. Ask: *What verb goes with photo B?* (Answer: *whistle*).

A yawn   B whistle   C scream   D laugh   E shout
F cry   G clap   H cheer

- Check meaning and pronunciation with students as you go through their answers.

3   In pairs, ask students to make the noises and get their partner to say what the noise is.

Listening

4   Explain that two people, Marion and Steve, have entered a radio phone-in competition to try to win a prize.
- Ask the class to read the three sentences and then listen to the recording to decide whether they are true or false.
- Play the tape again if necessary, before class feedback.

1 T   2 F   3 F

5   Now ask students to read the five questions then listen again for the answers.
- Let them check their answers in pairs before class feedback.

1 train station, airport, bus driver, taxi driver
2 bus driver
3 actor, musician, tennis player, football player
4 judo player
5 boxer

6   Ask the class to make a list of all the sounds they can remember from the recording. Put them into pairs to discuss this and then ask for class feedback. You may want to play the recording again or let students read the recording script to check.

Grammar focus

7   Ask the class to look at the examples and match them with their meanings.
- First do the example with the class.
- Finish with class feedback.

1 d   2 e   3 a   4 b   5 c

Practice

8   Ask the class to complete the sentences, following the example.

1 must be   2 might be   3 must be
4 can't be   5 A: must be   B: might be
6 can't be   7 must be   8 can't be

Get talking

9   Tell students they are going to take part in the radio phone-in competition they were listening to before.
- Play the recording and stop after each clue for them to follow the instructions.
- Then play the complete sequence to see if they have guessed the job correctly.
- Check their answers at each stage. Encourage them to use *must, might, can't.*

Hairdresser

10   Now get them to listen to the next sequence of sounds and repeat the process again, following the same instructions.

Waiter

Vocabulary Time expressions with *in, on, at* or no preposition
Grammar Present continuous for future time
Language to go Talking about future arrangements

A football fan's website

Language notes

• While we often teach that the present continuous is used for future plans and *going to* for 'decisions made before now', there is of course not a huge difference between the two concepts, and the forms are often interchangeable. The main thing is to get students away from the idea that *will* is the only future in English.

Way in

• Write on the board: *3:30   6:45   12:00   17:00   22:25 8:00 a.m.   7:00 p.m.*
• Divide the class into pairs to say each of the times. Remind them that there is often more than one way of saying the same time.

> 3:30 – three thirty / half past three / half three
> 6:45 – six forty-five / quarter to seven
> 12:00 – twelve o'clock / midday / midnight
> 17:00 – five o'clock / seventeen hundred hours
> 22:25 – ten twenty-five / twenty-five past ten / twenty-two, twenty-five
>
> 8:00 a.m. – eight o'clock / eight a.m. /ˌeɪ ˈem/
> 7:00 p.m. – seven o'clock / seven p.m. /ˌpiː ˈem/

Vocabulary

1 Students should be familiar with most of the time expressions, but may be less sure about which preposition goes with each.
• Go through the example, then students work in pairs putting the expressions in the correct columns.
• Class feedback – do this orally, or draw the table on the board and fill it in as you elicit the answers.

> in: *the morning / the afternoon / the evening*
> on: *Monday afternoon / Thursday*
> at: *10 a.m. / 6.45 p.m. / midnight / midday*
> no preposition: *tomorrow morning / last night / this Thursday / next Monday evening / yesterday morning / last Friday afternoon / this evening*

2 Students complete the sentences with the correct prepositions. Make it clear that sometimes they should leave the space blank.
• Class feedback.

> 1 at   2 no preposition   3 on   4 in   5 on   6 at
> 7 no preposition   8 no preposition

Reading and listening

3 Students look at the photo of Peter Gibson on page 74.
• Elicit that he is a Manchester United *fan* – he likes watching Manchester United football matches. He's organising a trip abroad for fans to follow a Manchester United tour, and information about this is on his web page.
• Go through the questions, then students read the web page and answer them.
• Class feedback.

> 1 Malaysia, Singapore, Thailand   2 3   3 11 days

Background information
Manchester United is a very successful English football team. They have won a lot of English and European competitions. They have a reputation for having fans all over the world, so whatever country they play in, they get local support.

4 Explain that there are some changes to the plans in the web page, and Peter is phoning another fan to explain the changes.
• Students look at the web page and change it as they listen.
• You may need to play the recording more than once.

Friday 20th	10.00	Leave London Heathrow
Saturday 21st	04.00	Arrive in Kuala Lumpur
	19.00	Group dinner at hotel
Saturday 22nd	10.00	Sightseeing tour by taxi
	21.00	Man Utd vs Malaysian Allstars at Bukit Jalil Stadium
Monday 23rd	09.00	Group dinner at Hilton
Tuesday 24th	10.00	Shopping
	20.00	Man Utd vs Singapore League XI – National Stadium
Thurs 26th–Sat 28th		Sightseeing, group meals, etc.
Sunday 29th	18.30	Man Utd vs Thailand National Team
Monday 30th	05.00	Return flight to UK
	11.00	Arrive at London Heathrow

Grammar focus

5 Ask students to underline the correct words to complete the explanations.

> 1 a definite future arrangement   2 need to

Practice

6 Students write five sentences about the trip, using the information in Exercise 4.
• Do the example before they start.
• Let pairs compare answers. Then ask for class feedback.

Get talking …

7 Tell students they are going to arrange a game of football with their friends.
• Get them to look at the diary page and make a time for the match, then try to get together a team of eleven people to play together.
• Get them to follow the instructions in their books very carefully, step by step.
• Once they have decided a date and completed their own diaries, get them to go around the class to find four people who are free to join the game. The winner is the first to complete their team.

… and writing

8 Ask students to write notes to help arrange a football match with another friend.
• Get them to follow the instructions in the book, first writing an invitation note to give to another student and then writing a reply note.
• You may wish to use the photocopiable models in the Writing bank (page 151) to focus on the conventions of writing short notes.

37

Adjectives

Vocabulary Adjectives and their opposites
Grammar *So* + adjective / *such* + noun
Language to go Emphasising feelings and opinions

It was so funny!

Language notes

- *So* and *such* are different forms with the same meaning, and so can be easily confused, e.g. ~~It was a so delicious meal.~~ [... *such a* ...]
- At this level we feel it's best not to go into the more complex construction *so*/*such* ... *that*..., e.g. *It was such a hard day that I'm exhausted.*
- *So* and *such* and any accompanying adjectives are usually strongly stressed and so are the adjectives that follow them. Exercises 5 and 6 focus students on this – encourage them to exaggerate the stress here to produce a natural stress pattern.

Way in

- Ask students in pairs to discuss what makes a good restaurant for them, and write down pairs of adjectives and nouns. Elicit/give a couple of examples to get them started, e.g. *nice food, friendly waiters.*
- Then ask them to discuss what a bad restaurant would be like, using opposite adjectives; again give them examples, e.g. *horrible food, unfriendly waiters.*
- Brief class feedback – you may want to list the opposites on the board for students to note down.

Vocabulary

1   • First ask students in pairs to put the correct adjectives in the first column. Tell them not to worry if they're not sure.
- Class feedback, checking pronunciation and meaning.
- Then students find the opposites and put them in the second column.
- Again, class feedback checking pronunciation and meaning.

> 1 full / hungry
> 2 great / terrible
> 3 funny / serious
> 4 attractive / ugly
> 5 ordinary / special
> 6 mean / generous

2   The aim here is to practise the vocabulary from Exercise 1.
- Explain that Tony is writing to Elisa about going to a restaurant with Miranda.
- Ask the class to read the letter and underline the correct adjectives in the letter.
- Do the example with the class.

> 1 special   2 funny   3 delicious   4 hungry
> 5 generous   6 great

Reading

3   Point out that the cartoon is numbered, and students should read from left to right across the two pages.
- Students read the cartoon, and discuss the question in pairs. Get pairs to explain the joke.
- Conduct brief class feedback.

4   Ask the class to look at the three sentences and then read the cartoon again.
- Then ask them to underline the correct words in the sentences, following the example.
- Do quick class feedback.

> 1 special   2 tired   3 boring

5   Ask students to listen to the conversation, and underline the stressed words in the cartoon.

> Glenda: That was <u>such</u> a terrible <u>day</u>. I'm <u>so</u> tired. How about <u>you</u>?
> Jim: <u>Terrible</u>! But I'm feeling <u>generous</u>. Let's go <u>out</u> for once and <u>eat</u>.
> Glenda: I'm <u>sorry</u> I was <u>so</u> long.
> Jim: No <u>problem</u>. That's an attractive <u>dress</u>.
> Glenda: <u>Thanks</u>.
> Glenda: Where are we <u>going</u>?
> Jim: To my <u>favourite</u> restaurant. You'll <u>love</u> it ... The food is <u>delicious</u>.
> Glenda: I'm <u>so</u> <u>hungry</u>.
> Jim: Me <u>too</u>.
> Glenda: Oh Jim. I work with <u>such</u> boring people. And I've been <u>so</u> <u>busy</u> at work. I'm <u>so</u> <u>tired</u>.
> Jim: Me <u>too</u>.
>   We're going to have <u>such</u> a <u>great</u> <u>evening</u>. Let's <u>relax</u> and <u>enjoy</u> it.

6   Students practise the dialogue in pairs, paying attention to stress and intonation.

Grammar focus

7   Get students to look at the example and read the explanation. Ask them to decide if the explanation is true or false.
- Go through the structures, pointing out when we use *so* and *such*, and when we need to add an article.

> True

Practice

8   Ask the class to complete the sentences using *so* or *such*, following the example.

> 1 so   2 such   3 such   4 so   5 so   6 such   7 so

Get talking

9   Ask students to read through the five experiences and choose two or three to talk about at first.
- In pairs, get them to explain why each of the personal experiences they have chosen was so special. They can talk about as many as time will allow.
- Get each student to decide which of their partner's experiences was most interesting. Then ask a few students to tell the class.

Vocabulary Immigration
Grammar Present perfect with *for/since*
Language to go Talking about how long you have done things

Green card

Language notes

- Although students will be familiar with the present perfect, this may be the first time they have studied this concept of it (something which started in the past and continues up to now), and the use of *for* and *since*.
- In some languages the present simple is used to express this concept, leading to a common error: ~~I am here for three months.~~ [*I've been here for three months*]. This can lead to misunderstandings, as it could be understood to refer to the future, rather than the past up to now.
- It's common for students to confuse *for* and *since*, but in fact often this will not impede communication: ~~I've lived here since three months~~ [*for*].

Way in

- Write or say: *What problems can you have at immigration and customs at an airport?*
- Pairs discuss the question, followed by a quick class discussion.

Possible answers
Problems at immigration: no visa, incorrect passport, not enough money, you might want to get a job.
Problems at customs: too many things you haven't paid tax on (e.g. alcohol, cigarettes, presents), smuggling things into the country.

Vocabulary

1 Students complete the text with words from the box. Tell them not to worry about words they're not sure of.
   - Students compare answers in pairs followed by class feedback. Check pronunciation and meaning.

1 immigration	2 ID card	3 driving licence
4 work permit	5 residence permit	6 green card

Cultural information
In many countries people have to carry *ID cards*. At the time of writing, British people don't have ID cards. The most common document used for identification in the UK is *a driving licence*.

Reading and listening

2 Students read the notes quickly to find out why the immigration officer is interviewing Kate and Rod Bolton.

To make sure the marriage is real.

3 Now ask the class to complete the table using the information in the text. Explain that this information is Rod's information only.
   - Show them the example before they start.
   - Finish with class feedback.

1 San Francisco	2 6 months ago	3 at a party
4 3 months ago	5 dance teacher	6 yes

4 📼 Tell the class that they are going to listen to the interview between US immigration and Kate.
   - Explain that her information is different from Exercise 3.
   - Students listen and complete Kate's information in the table.
   - Students compare which information is different. Class feedback.

1 Los Angeles: *different*	4 3 months ago
2 4 months ago: *different*	5 dance teacher
3 at a party	6 no: *different*

Grammar focus

5 Students read the examples and answer the three questions.
   - Check answers with the class.
   - You may want to revise the form of the present perfect, and reinforce the use of *for* for a period of time, and *since* for a point in time.

1 8 months ago	2 8 months ago	3 yes

Practice

6 Students write the expressions in the two columns.
   - Do the first two as examples.
   - Finish with class feedback.

For	Since
ages	May
two years	last summer
a couple of days	Friday
nine months	2001
	4 a.m.

7 Explain that this is part of Rod's interview.
   - Ask students to complete the dialogue between Rod and the immigration investigator with the correct form of the verbs.
   - Let pairs compare answers, but do not have any feedback yet.

8 📼 Ask the class to listen and check their answers.

1 've had	2 for	3 have you lived	4 Since
5 has she been	6 Since	7 have you known	8 For
9 you've been	10 since	11 have	12 hasn't been
13 since	14 hasn't		

Then ask them to practise the dialogue in Exercise 8 in pairs.

Get talking

9 This activity is a variation on 'Alibis'. A couple are interviewed separately by immigration officers, who are trying to find discrepancies in their stories and so establish that they are lying.
   - Round the class, label students A, B, C, D.
   - Students turn to their relevant pages. A and B are a married couple, C and D are immigration officers and are going to interview the couple separately.
   - Give students five minutes to prepare, using the prompts provided – immigration officers prepare their questions, and couples prepare their stories.
   - Put students in pairs, AC and BD. They carry out their interviews, but without listening to other pairs! You may want to move the pairs away from each other.
   - After the interviews, couples get back together and check whether they gave the same answers. Immigration officers get back together and compare notes – if the couple's stories differ, one of them must be lying!
   - Class feedback – ask each pair of immigration officers to deliver their 'verdict' to the class and explain it. How many couples were lying?

Vocabulary Nouns and verbs: word building
Function Making and responding to suggestions
Language to go Suggesting solutions to problems

Problem solving

Language notes

- In this lesson we focus on five forms for making suggestions, divided into three groups, according to their form:
  Why don't we, *Shall we* are questions, and are followed by an infinitive without *to*: *Why don't we tell him the truth?*
  Let's is also followed by an infinitive without *to*, but is not a question: *Let's sell the flat.*
  What about, *How about* are questions, followed by the *-ing* form: *What about asking him to dinner?*
- In the lesson we focus on nouns ending in *-tion*; these nouns (and those ending in *-cian*, *-sion*, *-sian*) are stressed on the syllable BEFORE the final syllable: e.g. *an invitation, a solution, a suggestion.*
  Two-syllable verbs are often stressed on the final syllable: e.g. *to invite, to suggest, to complain* (but *to visit*).
- You may want to encourage students to record new vocabulary in word families where possible: e.g.

Verbs	Nouns
invite	*invitation*
suggest	*suggestion*
solve	*solution*

Way in

Ask students what problems they have learning English. You may want to prompt with some ideas, e.g. remembering vocabulary, pronunciation, difficulties with listening.
- Students work in small groups, discuss their problems and suggest solutions.
- Get groups to report back to the class with their problems and solutions.

Vocabulary

1 Explain that Exercise 1 is about word formation, i.e. making nouns from verbs. Show them what you mean in the first example. Remind students that sometimes the verb and the noun in a word family are the same (as in the example here) and sometimes they are different.
- Check the answers together.

1 invitation   2 complaint   3 solution   4 lie
5 suggestion

2 📟 Write *suggestion* on the board. Ask them how many syllables there are. Ask *Which is the strongest syllable, one, two* or *three*? Say *suggestion*, emphasising the stress on the second syllable, and let the class repeat it. Then tell them to listen and repeat the nouns they hear. Pause the recording after each word to give students time to speak. You may need to play it twice. Point out that nouns that end in *-tion* are stressed on the syllable BEFORE the final syllable.

Listening

3 📟 Ask students to describe the pictures in pairs and guess the situation in each one. Now tell students they are going to listen to two conversations and match these to the correct pictures.

A Jane and Tom   B Jack and Becky

4 Check students understand that Jack and Becky live in the same house, and that Dan is staying with them.
- Students read the questions, then listen and answer the questions.
- Go through the answers with the class.

1 Two months ago
2 A week
3 They want him to leave
4 Say Jack's brother is coming / tell the truth

5 Tell students that they are now going to listen to Tom and Jane's problem.
- Students read the questions and listen for the answers.
- Check answers with the class.

1 The dog next door wakes the baby.
2 Yes, and he said he was going to take the dog to training classes.
3 Invite the neighbour for dinner / buy him a book on dog psychology / sell the flat.

Language focus

6 Ask students to look at the ways of making suggestions and of responding to suggestions too.
- Students match the sentence halves to complete the explanations. Point out that *Let's* … is not a question and so has no question mark.
- Remind students of the need for appropriate intonation when making and responding to suggestions. You may wish to get students to repeat the examples for practice.

1 b   2 a

Practice

7 There are two parts to this exercise.
- First ask students to complete the six suggestions on the left. Point out that there is more than one possible answer here.
- Check answers with the class.
- Next get students to match the completed suggestions on the left with the responses on the right.
- Check answers.

2 *Shall we / Why don't we* – d
3 *Shall we / why don't we / let's* – a
4 *Shall we / Why don't we* – b
5 *How about / What about* – f
6 *How about / What about* – e

8 Ask students to practise the dialogues with a partner, focusing on intonation.

Get talking and writing

9 Ask the class to read situation A and situation B. Check they all understand what is happening.
- Pairs discuss the problems and agree on a suitable suggestion for solving the problem. Then get them to write down the suggestion they have agreed on. Monitor and help where necessary.
- Students exchange their suggestions with another pair.
- Get them to write their responses, and finally return their response to the first pair.
- Ask students to report back to the class for feedback. Which suggestions were the best?

Vocabulary Parties
Grammar Second conditional (*if* + past simple + *would*/*could*)
Language to go Talking about imaginary situations

Celebrate

Language notes

- The second conditional describes an imaginary situation, how things might be different: *If I had a lot of money, I'd buy a bigger house* (I haven't got a lot of money, I can't buy a bigger house.).
- *Would* is introduced in Lesson 30, and is not too difficult for students to grasp. However, the use of the past simple in the *if* clause can be confusing. You need to make it clear that we are not actually talking about the past here, but an imaginary present, e.g. *If I had a lot of money ...* (now) or an imaginary future, e.g. *If I won the lottery ...* (next Saturday). The past simple here equates to a subjunctive form in many languages.
- Pronunciation: The contracted form of *would* (*I'd*, *he'd she'd*, etc.) is often not easy for students to hear, which can lead them to use the present simple rather than *would*, e.g. ~~If I had a lot of money, I buy a bigger house.~~ [*I'd buy ...*].

Way in

- Point out that this is the last lesson of the course.
- Ask students in small groups to think of ways of celebrating the end of the course.
- Finally, compare ideas and decide which ones are practical. You may actually want to act on one of the suggestions!

Vocabulary

1 Write three columns on the board. Get students to put the words in the box in the correct column under *drink*, *party* or *music*.
   - First do the example and then go through the exercise with the class, asking them to write up their answers on the board.

   DRINK – soft drink, alcohol-free beer, wine, champagne, lager
   PARTY – fancy dress, birthday, beach, dinner
   MUSIC – a live band, rock, jazz, salsa

2 Students use the vocabulary from Exercise 1 to complete the sentences. Show them the example first. Check the answers together.

   1 rock   2 soft drinks   3 alcohol-free beer   4 dinner
   5 wine   6 birthday

Reading

3 Explain that students are going to read an advert for a competition in a magazine.
   - Ask students to read the poster and answer the four questions.

   1 To celebrate the 100th edition of the magazine.
   2 Plan a party that you would like to have for someone.
   3 The magazine will pay for your party.
   4 Sixteen or over.

4 Ask students to look at the pictures and briefly describe the two situations. (Two people are imagining what kind of party they could have.)
   - Explain that they are going to read six sentences and decide who said each one, A or B.
   - Get them to match the sentences with the right person, following the example.

   1 A   2 A   3 B   4 A   5 A   6 B

Grammar focus

5 Ask students to look at the examples and underline the correct word to complete the explanation.

   imaginary

   - Use concept questions to reinforce the meaning, e.g. *Does she have a live band? (no) Is everyone dancing? (No, she's imagining it.) Is money a problem? (Yes) Are they having a party on a yacht? (No, she's imagining it.)*
   - You may wish to highlight the form on the board: *If* + past simple, *would*

6 Ask the class to listen and repeat the examples from Exercise 5.
   - Stop the recording after each sentence to give students time to repeat. Make sure students are hearing, and saying, contracted forms such as *I'd*, not just *I*.

Practice

7 Explain that they have to write sentences using the second conditional structure.
   - Do the first one as an example with the class.
   - Go through the answers.

   1 If Lenny didn't work in London, he'd live in the country.
   2 I wouldn't have to share a bedroom if I didn't have a sister.
   3 She'd give up work if she didn't need the money.
   4 If Jacob didn't have three children, he'd have a motorbike.
   5 I'd send you e-mails if you used your computer more often.

Get talking

8 Ask the class to imagine that they are going to enter the competition advertised in the magazine advert on page 82.
   - In pairs, students look back at the advert. Get them to discuss and write down their answers to the questions.
   - Students tell the rest of the class their ideas.
   - Ask the class to vote for the best idea.

Photocopiable material

Grammar Past simple (regular and irregular)
Language to go Talking about past events

Biography jigsaw

Aim

To practise asking and talking about past events

Materials

One copy of Sheet A and Sheet B per pair of students

Time

25 minutes

Preparation

Copy and cut Sheets A and B as above

Procedure

1 Divide the class into pairs (A+B).
2 Tell students they are going to look at a man's biography, but they will need to work together and exchange information to complete it.
3 Write the following sentences on the board as examples:
   In ____ , he bought a house.
   In 1985, he _____ .
   He went to _____ in 1987.
   Elicit the questions needed to obtain the missing information.
   When did he buy a house?
   What did he do in 1985?
   Where did he go in 1987?
4 Give students the relevant sheets and allow a suitable time limit to complete their parts of the lifeline. Tell them that they will find it easier if they ask the questions in the order they are numbered.
5 Give feedback, either as a whole class, or in different pairs (A+A, B+B).

Extension

Speaking: In pairs, students discuss possible answers to the following questions:
1 Why did he quit his job in 1996?
2 What happened to him in 2001?
3 Where is he now?

Sheet A

He was born in

London in (2) _____ .

He started school in 1966.

He won (4) _____ in 1977.

He finished school and went to university in 1979.

He (6) _____ in 1982.

He moved to New York in (7) _____ and worked there for

five years.

In 1995, he had a car accident.

The following year, he (10) _____ .

In 1996 and 1997, he travelled around the world. In (12) _____ ,

he met the Dalai Lama.

He decided that he wanted to change his life.

In 1998, he sold everything he owned and then (14) _____ .

After that, he lived (15) _____ and read many books.

In 2001, he disappeared.

Sheet B

He was born in (1) _____ in 1961.

He started school in (3) _____ .

He won the school prize in 1977.

He (5) _____ in 1979.

He left university and found a job in a bank in 1982.

He moved to New York in 1989 and worked there for

(8) _____ years.

In (9) _____ , he had a car accident.

The following year, he left his job.

In 1996 and 1997, he (11) _____ . In India, he met the Dalai Lama.

He decided that he wanted to change his life.

In 1998, he sold (13) _____ and then gave away all his money.

After that, he lived in the mountains and (16) _____ .

In 2001, he disappeared.

 © Pearson Education 2002

Vocabulary Free time activities
Grammar Likes / dislikes + -ing form + qualifying adjectives
Language to go Saying how much you like doing things

I really love holidays!

Aim

To practise talking about free time activities, using *love*, *like*, *hate* + -*ing* form of verbs, plus adverbs *really* and *quite*

Materials

One copy of Sheets A, B and C per group of three students

Time

25 minutes

Preparation

Cut and copy Sheets A, B and C as above

Procedure

1 Revise the verbs and adverbs by drawing a line on the board marked with either words or smiley faces.

| (really) love | like | (quite) like | don't like | hate | really hate |

2 Ask students to think if they like the same things as other members of their families. Give examples for yourself, e.g. *My brother and I both like X, I like Y but my sister likes Z, I like X but she hates it.* Ask students to discuss their ideas in small groups.

3 Ask students what the most important things are for two people, such as friends, to get on well together. Elicit similar interests and habits.

4 Divide the class into groups of three. You may have to have one or two pairs if the class doesn't divide evenly.

5 Explain that six boys are going on holiday together and that their task is to match people to share rooms. They have each interviewed two people and now they must compare notes and come to a conclusion about who should share with who.

6 Give each student in the group either Sheet A, B or C. If you have one or more pairs, divide Sheet C between Charlie and Dave and give half to Student A and half to Student B. Students exchange information with their partners, noting new information on their sheet.

7 Students now decide who should share with who. Give them some expressions for making suggestions (e.g. *What / How about ... , I think / don't think ...*) and emphasise that they need to explain their reasons.

8 Have a class feedback session to compare how different groups have paired the boys.

Extension

Speaking: Ask students which of the six they would be happiest sharing with.

SUGGESTED ANSWER
Adam with Eddie as both like films and dislike sport.
Ben with Fred as both like IT, dislike exercise and are quite untidy!
Charlie with Dave as they like getting up at the same time, have similar music tastes and Dave can cook for Charlie!

Sheet A

	love	like	doesn't like	hate
Adam	(go) cinema	all music	(drive) (play) sport	(watch) TV football
Ben				
Charlie				
Dave	(watch) TV football	the news (cook)	modern music	(get up) early
Eddie				
Fred				

Sheet B

	love	like	doesn't like	hate
Adam				
Ben	computers	(be) untidy (win)	(shop) cinema, theatre	(get up) at any time!
Charlie				
Dave				
Eddie	(get up) early	(do) yoga (watch) films	(write) e-mails team sports	rock and pop
Fred				

Sheet C

	love	like	doesn't like	hate
Adam				
Ben				
Charlie	classical music	(get up) late (play) sport	(be) tidy (cook)	(lose) at games
Dave				
Eddie				
Fred	the Internet	cars (watch) TV	(read) newspapers (tidy) room	(do) exercise

Vocabulary Weather, clothes and seasons
Grammar Present simple and continuous
Language to go Comparing usual and present situations

Dress code

Aim

To practise talking about climate and clothes and comparing temporary present actions with usual actions

Materials

One copy of the sheet per group of four students

Time

25 minutes

Preparation

Copy the sheet as above and cut each one into four pictures and four texts

Procedure

1 Tell the class to close their eyes. Select two students and ask the class to tell you what they are wearing. Alternatively, first ask two students to leave the room and then ask the others to describe what the two outside are wearing. Have the students open their eyes or bring the two back in to see if the class was correct. Ask the two students to compare what they are wearing today with what they wear in other seasons.

2 Divide the class into groups of four and give each student one of the pictures. If you have a group of three, just omit one picture.

3 Students then describe their picture to the others in the group.

4 Hand out the descriptions of the people, ensuring no one has the same person as their picture.

5 Students read the texts and guess who has the picture of what their person is wearing/doing today.

6 When they have matched the pictures and texts, they take the correct picture and think about what the person usually wears.

7 Finally, they tell the group as much as they can about what the weather is usually like and what their person usually wears compared with what the weather is like today and what the person is wearing. Others in the group can contribute ideas.

Extension

Speaking: In their groups, students compare what they are wearing today with what they wear in other seasons or situations (e.g. work, going out).

Writing: Step 7 can be written up for homework.

Mandy is an English teacher
in cold, snowy Oslo.
She enjoys her job, but is
very happy now, as it is
summer and she is relaxing
on holiday in Greece.

Paula works in a bar in hot,
dry Spain. She works all
summer in Ibiza in a bar on
the beach. Now it is spring,
and she is visiting her
parents in Ireland.

Susie is a web designer
from warm, sunny
Los Angeles. She loves
working at home and for
herself. Today it is winter,
and she is visiting a client
in Canada.

Jean works in a bank in cool,
cloudy London. She is very
traditional. Today is
Sunday. It is autumn and
she is staying with friends
in the countryside.

Vocabulary Possessions
Grammar Possessive 's, possessive adjectives / pronouns, *belong to*
Language to go Talking about what belongs to us

This is Mick's tie!

Aim

To practise language used for talking about possessions (possessive 's, possessive pronouns and *belong to* + object)

Materials

One copy of the sheet per group of four students
Slips of paper for the extension activity

Time

30 minutes

Preparation

For each group of four students, copy and cut the sheet into four biography cards, four summary tables and sixteen object cards

Procedure

1 Put students into groups of three or four and distribute one set of object cards to each group.
2 Students help each other to identify and name the sixteen objects. Conduct class feedback and correct pronunciation where necessary.
3 Give each student a 'likes / dislikes' table.
4 Distribute the four biography cards. Students take it in turns to read each one and summarise the important facts on their table. They then place the biography cards in a line on the desk.
5 With whole class, check vocabulary and conduct comprehension checks (e.g. *What type of person is Mick? What does Mary enjoy?*). Meanwhile, have each group shuffle the object cards and divide them between the three / four of them.
6 Students then take it in turns to place each of their object cards under the biography card of the person they think it belongs to, explaining why (e.g. *I think this is Mick's tie / This tie belongs to Mick because ...*). Others in the group can agree or disagree.
7 When students have placed all the cards, tell them that there should be four objects for each person and that they should try to agree on what belongs to whom.
8 Groups compare how they divided the possessions and why.

Extension

Writing: In the same groups, students write four favourite possessions of their own on slips of paper and pass them all to another group, who pick them one by one and guess who in the other group wrote it.

SUGGESTED ANSWER KEY

John: tie, dictionary (*works in foreign exchange dept*), mobile phone (*spends a lot of time speaking to friends*), hockey stick (*likes team sports*).

Mick: magazine (*goes to a lot of concerts/ films*), bag (*carries books about*), CD (*likes music*), laptop (*takes work home*).

Mary: guitar (*wants to be in a band*), TV (*likes relaxing at home*), trainers (*likes doing exercise*), mini-disc player (*likes music*).

Janet: watch (*likes water sports*), radio (*travels/ likes the news*), camera, teapot (*likes Chinese food/ doesn't drink alcohol*).

This is Mick's tie!

John
John, 29, works in a bank, in the foreign exchange department. He likes the excitement in his job. He lives alone in a flat, but doesn't spend much time there. He is very sociable and spends a lot of time talking to his friends. After work, he likes going out, and at weekends he plays a lot of team sports. He loves champagne, but doesn't really like coffee.

Mick
Mick, 36, is a language teacher in a secondary school. He is married and has two daughters. He is very kind. He works very hard and often has to take his work home in the evenings. He likes music, but can't play any. At weekends, he goes to concerts, the opera or to the cinema. He likes romantic films and hates action movies.

Mary
Mary, 24, is a designer. She shares a flat with her friend. She has just started her first job so she doesn't have much money. She loves cooking dinner for her friends and relaxing at home. She loves exercise and keeping fit but hates competitive sports. When she goes out, she goes clubbing and to rock concerts. She would like to be in a band.

Janet
Janet, 31, works in a travel agent's. She likes her job because she gets lots of cheap holidays. Her favourites are beach holidays and activity/adventure trips. She often goes swimming and does a lot of water sports. She likes Chinese food and coffee but doesn't drink alcohol. She reads a lot. She can live without music, but never misses the news.

	Likes	Dislikes
John		
Mick		
Mary		
Janet		

	Likes	Dislikes
John		
Mick		
Mary		
Janet		

	Likes	Dislikes
John		
Mick		
Mary		
Janet		

	Likes	Dislikes
John		
Mick		
Mary		
Janet		

Vocabulary Weddings
Grammar *Should/ shouldn't* and imperatives
Language to go Giving advice

Dinner party

Aim

To practise giving advice using *should* and *shouldn't* and to talk about going to someone's house for dinner

Materials

One copy each of Sheets A, B and C

Time

25 minutes

Preparation

Cut and copy Sheets A, B and C as above (for larger classes, make two copies and have six groups)

Procedure

1 Find out how often students have dinner with friends.
2 Ask the class if they prefer going to a restaurant or to someone's house for dinner, and briefly discuss pros and cons. Teach *have/ give a dinner party*, *guest*, *host*.
3 Tell the class that they are going to prepare some advice for someone who is going to someone's house for dinner for the first time.
The person has met the hosts before, but does not know them well.
4 Divide the class into three groups: A, B and C. For larger classes, have six groups (two of each). Explain that Group A should write advice on what to do and what not to do before the meal, Group B on advice for during the meal, and Group C should focus on advice for after the meal.
5 Give them the relevant sheet with ideas, and a time limit, for example ten minutes.
6 Monitor and help as needed. All members of the group should write the sentences.
7 When they have finished writing, organise them into groups of three (A+B+C).
8 They then take it in turns to read and discuss their sentences.

Extension

Speaking: Ask the students to talk about any special meals they have had.

Before you eat

Think about what someone should or shouldn't do when they arrive and before the meal. Write some advice using your own ideas or the ideas below.

- Arrive: early, on time, ten minutes late, half an hour late?
- Clothes: smart, casual, jeans, dinner jacket?
- What if you have a problem and are going to be late?
- Take your shoes off or leave them on?
- Go into the kitchen and help cook? Talk to other guests? Read the paper? Ask to watch the news on TV? Look around the house?
- Sit anywhere you want at the table?

While you eat

Think about what someone should or shouldn't do during the meal.
Write some advice using your own ideas or the ideas below.

- Smoke?
- Conversation topics: the food, politics, religion, yourself?
- Serve yourself or wait for the host to serve you?
- Eat in silence, talk a little, talk all the time?
- Eat everything or leave some food on your plate? Ask for more? Help yourself?
- Eat and drink quietly or make some eating and drinking noises?

After you eat

Think about what someone should or shouldn't do after the meal.
Write some advice using your own ideas or the ideas below.

- Comments on the food: say nothing, say what you really thought, say that it was lovely?
- Offer to wash up? Suggest watching football on TV while the host washes up?
- Ask for the recipe of something good you ate?
- Fall asleep?
- Leave: immediately, after 30 minutes, after two to three hours, stay all night?
- Say thank you: when (that evening, the next day)? How (by phone, letter, fax, email)?

Vocabulary Countries and continents
Grammar The future with *going to*
Language to go Talking about future plans

All around the world

Aim

To practise talking about future plans using *going to*, and language for countries and continents

Materials

One copy of the sheet per pair of students

Time

25–30 minutes

Preparation

Copy the sheet as above

Procedure

1 Ask the students if they ever enter competitions and if they have ever won anything.
2 Explain that for this activity, they are going to enter a competition to win a trip around the world. To take part, they have to plan their ideal trip. The winners will be the ones who plan the best trip.
3 Explain the rules:
   • The trip must be three to twelve months long.
   • They must visit each of the five continents and can visit only one country in each continent.
   • They must keep moving in the same direction around the world.
4 Divide the class into pairs.
5 Give each pair a copy of the sheet and fifteen minutes to plan their route. They should think about why they want to visit each country, what they want to see and do there, how and where they want to travel within it, what they want to buy there, how long they want to stay.
6 They mark the route on the map and then work together to complete the written description. Monitor and assist as required.
7 When all the plans have been written, collect them in and stick them up around the room.
8 Students move about individually reading each one and finally vote on the trip that they think is the most interesting (this can be done by ticking the bottom of the sheet). Students cannot vote for their own.
9 Count the ticks and declare the winner!

Extension

Speaking: Ask the students what real travel plans they have.

Our trip

First of all we are going to fly to _____ in _____ . We are going to stay _____

weeks / months and while we are there, we are going to _____

_____ and we are going to

_____

Next, we are going to spend _____ in _____ .

We are going to go there so / because we _____

_____ and we are going to

_____

The third country _____ visit is _____ in _____ .

We _____ because _____

_____

_____

Then we _____

_____

_____

_____

Finally _____

_____

_____

_____

Verbs you could use: travel   visit   see   look at   buy   do   take   stay   go to

Vocabulary Adjectives to describe character
Grammar Comparatives
Language to go Making comparisons

Comparison cards

Aim

To practise language of comparisons using *-er than*, *more ... than*, *not as ... as* and adjectives of behaviour

Materials

One set of cards per pair of students

Time

25 minutes

Preparation

Copy the sheet as above, on card if possible, and cut into two sets of eighteen cards. It would be helpful to have the adjective cards and people cards on different-coloured card. For example, copy the page onto blue and red card and give half the pairs blue 'adjectives' and red 'people', and vice versa for the others.

Procedure

1 Divide class into pairs.
2 Review vocabulary if necessary.
3 Give each pair one set of 'adjective' cards and one set of 'people' cards in piles face down.
4 Ask them to shuffle each pile.
5 In pairs, students take turns to pick a card from the top of each pile and compare themselves to the person or people on the 'people' card using the adjective on the 'adjective' card. They should use one of the target structures (e.g. *I am more talkative than my brother/I am not as talkative as my brother*). If the 'people' card is not relevant (e.g. a student does not have a brother/sister/partner), he/she can replace the card in the pile and draw another one.
6 Encourage students to give a reason where possible and encourage their partners to respond. In a class where students know each other well, they could say if they agree or disagree.

Extension

Writing: Students write some of the sentences for homework.

talkative	co-operative	noisy
aggressive	messy	romantic
hardworking	lazy	friendly
tidy	calm	intelligent
competitive	shy	happy
emotional	good-looking	kind

brother / sister	most of my friends	the teacher of this class
my boss / teachers at school / university	partner (husband / wife / girlfriend / boyfriend)	most people in my country
best friend	most of my relatives	most people my age
mother	grandparents	my cat / dog / pet
father	classmates	me ten years ago
a typical woman	a typical man	you

Vocabulary Adventure sports
Grammar Present perfect and past simple
Language to go Talking about past experiences

What an experience!

Aim

To practise talking about past experiences using present perfect and past simple and vocabulary related to adventurous sports

Materials

One set of cards per group of four students

Time

25 minutes

Preparation

Copy the sheet as above, cut into sets of cards and separate each set into two piles, each containing one of the two cards for each sport

Procedure

1 Divide the class into groups of four (or five, if four isn't possible, in which case there will be no spare cards on the table, and any pairs dealt to a student can immediately be deemed to have been won – see steps 4 and 5).

2 Give each group one pile of fifteen cards (which should contain one example of each of the fifteen sports) and ask them to work together to identify them all. Teach new vocabulary where necessary (e.g. *bungee jumping, parachuting, sky diving, hot-air ballooning*).

3 Tell students that they are going to play a card game which involves asking and speaking about *imaginary* experiences on cards given to them, and that the bottom of each card shows when the holder did it and his/her opinion of it. Demonstrate with one or two cards. In the game, if a student doesn't have a card for a particular activity, then he/she has never done it.

4 Put together sets of cards for each group, shuffle them well and deal out seven to each player, leaving two on the table.

5 Ask students to make sure that they do not have any two cards with the same sport on at this stage. If they do, they can swap either with a card on the table or with another player. If this is also a pair, they can make one more swap. If they *still* have a pair, they can put the pair on the table as if they had won it.

6 Students now take it in turns to ask any other member of their group if they have done an activity. If the student being asked doesn't have the card, he/she says so.
Student A: *Have you ever ... ?*
Student B: *No, I haven't.*
Play then passes to the student to the left of Student A.

7 If Student A asks Student B for a card and the answer is *Yes*, they should develop the conversation. Demonstrate with one student:
T: *Have you ever ... ?*
S: *Yes, I have.*
T: *Really? So have I! When did you do it?*
S: *In 1999.*
T: *What was it like?/What did you think of it?*
S: *I thought it was great.*
T: *That's funny, I didn't really like it.*
etc.

8 Student A takes the card from Student B, puts the pair down on the table and play passes to the person on Student A's left.

9 The game finishes when all the cards have been put down and the winner is the one with the most pairs.

10 As students play the game, monitor and check use of tenses.

Extension

Speaking: Find out which students have really done which of the activities.

8

What an experience!

1999 great	1998 wonderful	two years ago really good	many times fantastic	last year great
1997 fantastic	last month didn't like it	2001 frightening	in 2000 OK	1998 + 2000 fantastic
many times really enjoyed	at Christmas excellent	last April I didn't finish	on holiday awful	when student great
last week not bad	1999 superb	last summer very tough	four years ago fantastic	at school a bit boring
2001 hated it	last summer very nice	not sure didn't enjoy it	at school OK	years ago so-so
at university scary	few years ago a bit boring	when sixteen brilliant	six months ago quite good	1999 really good

Vocabulary At the office: verb + noun combinations
Function Offers and requests
Language to go Making and responding to offers and requests

E-mail favours

Aim

To practise making offers and requests at work using *Can/Could you … ?, I'll … , Shall I … ?* and office verb + noun combinations

Materials

One copy of the sheet per student (plus slips of paper for the extension)

Time

25 minutes

Preparation

Copy the sheet as above (or see Alternative)

Procedure

1 Ask students how often they use e-mail. If they are working, ask how many e-mails they send and receive each day. Pick two or three students and find out if their e-mails are mainly from colleagues or people outside the company. Elicit the differences there would be (much less formal with colleagues).
2 Tell students that they are going to read some e-mails.
3 Hand out a copy of the sheet to each student and ask them to scan it and tell you if the e-mails are internal or external. (Answer: internal and all informal. Note use of first names, or only initials, and informal requests and text-messaging abbreviations in e-mail 2 (*I'm going to be late … can you tell Mary for me?*).)
4 Ask students to work with a partner to match the requests (1–5) to the replies (6–10).
5 Now ask them to look at the four requests at the bottom of the page and to write suitable replies using some accepting/declining/offering/requesting language.

Alternative

With a stronger class, the activity could be made more challenging by cutting up all the e-mails (1–14) and getting students to identify requests and replies before matching them and writing replies to those without one.

Extension

Writing: Students think of other situations and write e-mails on slips of paper for the teacher to 'deliver' to other students who then write a reply.

> ANSWER KEY
> 1+9, 2+8, 3+6, 4+10, 5+7
>
> SAMPLE REPLIES
> 11 Yes, of course. Could you give me the details of where and when?
> 12 Yes, please. Shall I bring you back some chocolate?
> 13 No, I haven't, but pop it on my desk and I'll do it this afternoon.
> 14 Certainly – I'll do it straightaway.

9

E-mail favours

Match the requests (1–5) to the replies (6–10).

1 Michael We need to see Mr Xu and his team. Shall I arrange a meeting for early next week? P	**6** Sorry, I'm afraid I can't at the moment, as the machine is broken. We are waiting for someone to come and fix it. J
2 I'm going 2 B late for the meeting, can U tell Mary 4 me?	**7** No problem. Shall I do the same with the faxes? J
3 I have a lot of things to do today, so could you do some photocopying for me? Thanks	**8** Sure. I don't think it will start on time anyway.
4 Sarah I've just got a fax from Mr Ramos in Spain. Could you read it and translate it for me, please?	**9** Can you make it the week after? I need to write the report first. M
5 Jack I am away next week. If I get any important e-mails, can you forward them to me? Thanks, Brian	**10** Yes, of course. Do you want me to write the reply too? S

Now write a suitable reply to these requests and offers.

11 Could you write to Mr Patel to invite him to the meeting we are having next week? I think we need him to be there. H	**13** Dave Have you read the fax that William sent? Can you reply before 5.00 pm? Peter
12 Helen Have a good trip to Belgium. Shall I check your e-mail for you while you are away? Mark	**14** Simon Thanks for sending that letter to Filos Ltd. Could you fax it to them as well, as I am worried about the post?

 © Pearson Education 2002

Vocabulary Verbs and their opposites
Grammar Zero conditional (*if* + present form + present form)
Language to go Talking about consequences

What if ... ?

Aim

To practise zero conditionals

Materials

One copy of the sheet per group of three or four students

Time

25 minutes

Preparation

Copy the sheet as above and cut it into 30 cards

Procedure

1 Pre-teach any unknown vocabulary (e.g. *a queue*, *to leave a note*, *to remind someone*).
2 Divide the class into groups of three or four students.
3 Give each group a set of 30 cards (ten questions each cut into three parts).
4 Students work together to match the three parts of each question. Give them an example if necessary.
5 In groups, students discuss the answers to the questions.

Alternatives

• Begin by giving students just the first part of the questions (the *if* clause) and let them discuss possible endings before handing out the endings to match.
• Divide the slips of paper between students, up to three each, mixing *if* clauses and endings. Students then do a walkabout, trying to trade their endings to make complete questions.

Extension

Writing: Students write further questions.

What if … ?

If a waiter forgets to put some expensive drinks on your bill, …	Do you keep quiet and pay it?	Or do you remind him to add them?
If a shop assistant gives you too much change, …	Do you walk away and keep it?	Or do you tell him / her about the mistake and give it back?
If someone asks you how to get to somewhere near, …	Do you give them directions?	Or do you take them there yourself?
If you borrow something from a friend then lose / break it, …	Do you get him / her another one?	Or do you keep quiet and hope he / she forgets?
If a waiter brings you some food that is a bit too cold, …	Do you eat it?	Or do you send it back?
If people push into a queue in front of you, …	Do you say nothing and wait?	Or do you ask them to go to the back?
If your teacher forgets to give you some homework, …	Do you ask him / her for some?	Or do you go home and watch television?
If someone near you in a cinema makes a lot of noise, …	Do you ask them to be quiet?	Or do you move to another place?
If you hit another car when you are parking yours, …	Do you drive away?	Or do you leave a note?
If a friend asks to borrow some money to buy a lottery ticket, …	Do you lend him some?	Or say you haven't got any?

Vocabulary Customs: verb + noun combinations
Grammar *Used to / didn't use to*
Language to go Talking about past customs

When we were young

Aim

To practise *used to / didn't* use to to talk about past habits and customs

Materials

One copy of the sheet per student

Time

25 minutes

Preparation

Copy the sheet as above (if you are using the Alternative, you also need to cut out the thought bubbles (stuck on card if possible) so that there is one set for each group)

Procedure

1 Ask students to imagine someone who is now 100 years old. What was life like when they were a child? Jot down some ideas on the board (e.g. no TV, different clothes).
2 Give out the sheets and ask students to look at the picture. Ask a few questions: *How old do they look? When were they children?* Ask students what the couple are thinking about (their childhood) and elicit the necessary vocabulary.
3 Explain that students must imagine they are either the man or the woman. They have been asked to write an article for a magazine for young people about their childhood. This is to try to help young people learn about the past. As well as using the pictures, they can also add their own ideas.
4 Working individually, students write the article; monitor their work and help where necessary.
5 In pairs, they compare their answers. Ask one or two to read out their articles. Correction can either be done while monitoring or the articles can be handed in.

Alternative

After step 1, put students into groups of three or four. Give each group a set of thought bubbles, which they should put face down in the middle. In turns, each student turns over one of the cards and describes it to the rest of the group. When they have finished, ask them how similar life is now to the pictures and when they think life was like that. Now give them a copy of the sheet each and explain that the thought bubbles are the childhood memories of the couple in the picture. They then continue with the writing activity in step 3.

Extension

Speaking: Students talk about how life was different when they were children or they imagine they are 100 years old and interview each other about their childhoods.

Imagine you are the man or woman in the picture and you are writing about your childhood for a magazine for young people.

When we were young _____

_____

_____

_____

_____

Vocabulary Shops and purchases
Grammar *Because/for* and infinitive of purpose (with *to*)
Language to go Giving reasons

Going to town

Aim

To practise shop names and
*because/for/*infinitive of purpose

Materials

Two copies of the sheet per
group of four students

Time

30 minutes

Preparation

Copy the sheet as above and cut
up half the copies into sets of
twenty squares

Procedure

1 Divide students into groups of four (or another number if necessary,
but not multiples of three). Hand out one whole sheet per group.
2 Ask students to look at the pictures and think of the name of each
place. Do the first picture (*newsagent's*) as an example. Students
should write the names on the sheet.
3 Feedback from students to ensure they all have the correct names.
Check the spelling and pronunciation as they do this.
4 Ask students to put away the sheets and hand out the cut-up cards
(one set per group). Ask them to put the squares face down in a pile
in the middle of the group.
5 Write on the board:
1 *because*
2 *for*
3 *to* + verb
Ask students to take it in turns round their group to turn over the
squares and finish the sentence: *I went to the … because/for/to*
+ verb … They should rotate through the three forms, i.e. Student 1
makes a sentence with *because*, Student 2 with *for*, Student 3 with
to + verb, Student 4 with *because*, Student 1 with *for,* etc.
6 They should try to remember the place names without referring to
their complete sheet. If the other students think that the sentence is
correct, the student keeps the square. If not, they put it back at the
bottom of the pile. They are not allowed to repeat a sentence that
another student has already said.
7 Ask a group to do a couple of examples to make sure everyone
understands what they have to do. While they are doing the activity,
monitor their work, check for mistakes and answer any
disagreements.
8 When students have finished, they should count how many squares
they have. The one with the most is the winner of the group.

Extension

Speaking: Memory chain game
1 Students sit in a circle round the class. Write the sentence *I went to
the town centre …* on the board.
2 Student 1 has to finish the sentence, e.g. *I went to the town centre
to meet my friend.*
3 Student 2 should then repeat what the first student said and add to it,
e.g. *I went to the town centre to meet my friend and because I
needed some stamps.*
4 Student 3 continues, e.g. *I went to the town centre to meet my
friend, because I needed some stamps and for a bottle of wine,* etc.
5 If a student makes a mistake, he/she is out. Continue until only one
student is left.

Vocabulary	Large numbers; hotel facilities
Grammar	*Have* and *have got*
Language to go	Facilities and regular activities

Room with a view

Aim

To practise *have* vs. *have got* and vocabulary of hotels / holidays

Materials

One copy of the sheet for each group of four students

Time

25–30 minutes

Preparation

Copy the sheet as above and cut into Sheets A and B

Procedure

1 Divide the board into two columns: one headed *The ideal holiday hotel* and the other *A terrible holiday hotel*. Elicit a couple of ideas of what for them is the ideal holiday resort (e.g. a nice pool, good rooms) and what is a terrible resort (e.g. a dirty pool, no bar). Elicit *it has got a view of …*

2 In pairs, students jot down some ideas. After five minutes, get feedback and write the points on the board.

3 Divide the class into pairs and nominate each pair A or B. Explain that they are all on holiday: the As are at a wonderful hotel and the Bs are at a terrible hotel. They have to write a postcard to a friend or a family member telling them about the hotel and their holiday. They should use *have / have got* where possible. (At this point, it is a good idea to ask them if a postcard is formal or informal; and when both *have* and *have got* are possible, which is more appropriate.)

4 Hand out the sheets (Sheet A to A pairs and Sheet B to B pairs). Ask students to look at the pictures and explain that these are to give them ideas, but that they can use their imagination as well. Using the pictures, elicit a couple of examples from both As and Bs. Make sure that you include at least one example of *have* as a dynamic verb, e.g. *have dinner, have a swim.*

5 Give students ten minutes to write their postcards, monitoring and helping where necessary.

6 When the students have finished, As should give their postcard to a pair of Bs to read and vice versa. The postcards can then be displayed on the walls. All students can go around the room reading them and then vote for 'The best holiday hotel' and 'The worst holiday hotel'.

7 Correction can either be done after this, or during monitoring, or by the students as they go around reading.

Extension

Speaking: In pairs, students describe hotels they have visited. While monitoring, watch out for the use of *have got* in the possessive sense – students may use the past and try to use **had** *got*. You may want to check that students are aware that the past form of *have got* in the sense of possession is just *had* (e.g. *The hotel has got a swimming pool* ➜ *The hotel had a swimming pool*).

Sheet A

Sheet B

Vocabulary Food and drink
Grammar *Some, any, much, many, a lot of*
Language to go Discussing what you eat and drink

World food

Aim

To practise food vocabulary and *some/any/much/many/a lot of*

Materials

One copy of the sheet per group of four students; additional pictures of food from magazines

Time

25–30 minutes

Preparation

Copy the sheets as above and cut them into Sheets A, B, C and D

Procedure

1 Pre-teach any food vocabulary in the texts that your students might not know.
2 Divide the class into groups of four (Students A, B, C and D in each group). Explain that they are each going to read about a person from a different country and his/her eating habits.
3 Draw this table on the board and ask students to copy it.

	Student A	Student B	Student C	Student D
Breakfast				
Lunch				
Dinner				
Typical food/dishes				
Drink				
Young people				

4 Hand out the appropriate sheet (A, B, C or D) to each student and give them seven minutes to read their text and complete as much of their part of the table as they can. Point out that they might not have information for all the rows. As they do this, monitor to help with any vocabulary problems.
5 Now ask students to tell the others in their group about the eating habits of the country they read about. While they listen to the other group members, they should complete as much of the rest of the table as possible. When each one has finished, they should discuss which country they think it might be.
6 When all students have finished, write the following countries on the board: *Brazil, Germany, Thailand, India, Japan, China, Spain, Poland.* In their groups, students should match each text to a country.
7 As follow-up, students could tell each other which of these foods they eat themselves.

Extension

If you have a multilingual class ask students to write a text about eating habits in their country, which can be displayed around the classroom for other students to read.

ANSWER KEY (MAIN TASK)
A = Japan   B = Spain   C = Thailand   D = Poland

Sheet A

In my house, we eat a lot of different types of fish and seafood, but we don't eat much meat. Older people don't drink much coffee in my country, but it is becoming popular with young people. Tea is the most popular drink. In the summer, it is hot and we drink a lot of beer. We also drink some alcohol which is made from rice. Now, foreign food is becoming more popular, and when we eat French or Italian food, we usually drink some wine. We don't use many spices or herbs in our cooking. Sandwiches are now more common in my country for lunch, and for breakfast; we often have an egg and some bread – or even some soup! We eat a lot of rice and some types of pasta, but not very many potatoes.

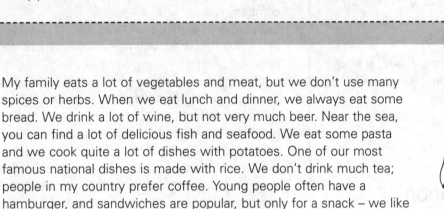

Sheet B

My family eats a lot of vegetables and meat, but we don't use many spices or herbs. When we eat lunch and dinner, we always eat some bread. We drink a lot of wine, but not very much beer. Near the sea, you can find a lot of delicious fish and seafood. We eat some pasta and we cook quite a lot of dishes with potatoes. One of our most famous national dishes is made with rice. We don't drink much tea; people in my country prefer coffee. Young people often have a hamburger, and sandwiches are popular, but only for a snack – we like to spend a lot of time over our meals. When we have a drink, we often eat some olives or crisps.

Sheet C

My family eats rice with every meal. We also eat some types of pasta. Sometimes, for breakfast, we have some bread and biscuits and drink some coffee, but not very often. There are many different dishes in my country – we eat a lot of vegetables, fish and seafood and we also eat some meat, especially chicken and pork. We use a lot of spices when we cook – foreigners think our food is very hot! We like to use some sauces with our food, usually spicy and sometimes made with fish. We don't eat much bread at home, but people sometimes buy hamburgers and sandwiches at fast-food restaurants, especially young people. We don't make any wine in my country, so it is quite expensive, but beer is very popular.

Sheet D

In my family, the most popular dish is meat with a lot of potatoes and vegetables. I don't eat any pasta, but I sometimes eat rice. We don't eat much spicy food in my house. For breakfast, we usually eat sandwiches and drink some coffee or tea. Sometimes at the weekend, I have a big breakfast with all my family and then we eat eggs with some bread and sometimes sausages, but we never eat any cereal. We have our main meal at about three o'clock – we usually have some soup and then a main course – potatoes, vegetables and some meat or some fish. We have a type of drink made with fruit and sometimes wine. Dinner is a light meal at about six or seven o'clock – we don't eat very much, just sandwiches.

Vocabulary British and American words for clothes
Grammar Past and present obligation with *have* / *had to*
Language to go Talking about obligation

Rules and regulations

Aim

To practise *have to* / *don't have to* for obligation

Materials

One copy of the sheet for each group of three / four students

Time

25 minutes

Preparation

Copy the sheet as above

Procedure

1 Put students into groups of three or four. Tell them that they are the Board of Directors of a new company and that they have to write the company rules.
2 Elicit areas at work which have rules and write them on the board (e.g. what you wear, when you work, where you work, what you do, how you behave).
3 In their groups, students decide what their company does and give it a name. You could give them some ideas, e.g. a bank, Internet company, fashion designers.
4 Hand out one sheet for each group and ask them to fill in the company name at the top.
5 Now ask students to decide on ten rules for their company and write them on the sheet with *have to* / *don't have to*. Elicit a couple of examples first, e.g. *You have to wear a suit*, *You don't have to come to work every day*. They can use the pictures to give them ideas. Monitor and help if necessary. Watch out for misuse of *don't have to* to mean *mustn't*, e.g. *You don't have to arrive late*.
6 As feedback, ask all or some of the groups to read out their rules.

Alternative

If you think your class has no / little experience of the workplace, you could ask them to write rules for a school / their language school instead.

Company / School name: ....

The rules

`11:37`

1 _____

2 _____

3 _____

4 _____

5 _____

6 _____

7 _____

8 _____

9 _____

10 _____

Grammar Future predictions with *will/won't*
Language to go Predicting the future

Crystal ball

Aim

To practise *will/won't* for predictions and *I think/I don't think + will*

Materials

One copy of the sheet per pair

Time

25–30 minutes

Preparation

Copy the sheet as above and cut into Sheets A and B

Procedure

1 Divide students into pairs and allocate each pair either A+A or B+B. Give each student a copy of the appropriate sheet.
2 Explain that they are going to ask each other about future predictions, both about their lives and life in general. Ask them to read their six questions and then give them time to ask questions about vocabulary.
3 Students work in pairs to write four extra questions to complete their questionnaire. At this point, monitor and correct if necessary.
4 Put students into new pairs (A+B).
5 Students now interview each other. Ask one strong pair to illustrate. Try to encourage the use of short answers and *I think/I don't think + will*. Students can make notes if they want.
6 Each student now reports to the class two interesting answers that their partner gave, e.g. *Jaime thinks that Spain will win the football World Cup. He doesn't think he will ever speak fluent English.*

Sheet A

Predictions

1 Who will win the next football World Cup?

2 Will you have children in the next five years?

3 When will people start living on the moon?

4 How long will you continue to study English for?

5 Will the UK ever have a president?

6 What clothes will people wear in the year 2100?

7 _____

_____

8 _____

_____

9 _____

_____

10 _____

_____

Sheet B

Predictions

1 Will you ever move to another country?

2 When will it be possible to travel from London to Australia in less than eight hours?

3 What will the weather be like at the weekend?

4 Will you speak fluent English in ten years' time?

5 What will people eat in the year 2500?

6 Will you ever write a book?

7 _____

_____

8 _____

_____

9 _____

_____

10 _____

_____

Vocabulary Adjectives describing places and objects; transport
Grammar Superlatives
Language to go Using superlatives to describe places

The best place in the world

Aim

To practise superlatives to talk about a city

Materials

One copy of the sheet per group of fourteen students (or per group, if following the Alternative)

Time

25 minutes

Preparation

Copy the sheet as above and cut it into fourteen cards

Procedure

1 Tell students that they are going to talk about the city/town where they are now. On the board write *Where/good/place to learn English?* to elicit the full question (*Where is the best place to learn English?*) and get a few answers.
2 If there are more than fourteen students in the class, divide them into two equal groups and adjust the number of cards in each set accordingly so that each group will have the same questions.
3 Give out one question card to each student. Ask them to look at their question and make sure they know how to form it. At this point, monitor and help if necessary.
4 Ask students to stand up and go around asking their classmates the answer to their question. While they are doing this, they should keep a tally of the different answers on the back of the question card. Monitor and check for mistakes.
5 As feedback, ask each student to read out his/her question and tell the class what some of the most popular answers were.
6 If you were working with two groups, get them to compare their answers.

Alternative

1 Put students into groups of three or four and give each group one set of cards.
2 Students take it in turns to read a card and ask their group the question. The whole group then discusses what they think the answer is. Then the next student takes the next card, etc.
3 As feedback, ask round the class what some of their answers were and see if they agree or disagree with each other.

What / popular / tourist / attraction?

What / expensive / restaurant?

Where / near / market?

What / unusual / place?

What / interesting / building?

What / trendy / clothes shop?

What / easy / way to meet new people?

Where / good / place to buy second-hand clothes?

What / good / thing about this place?

Which / busy / street?

What / cheap / thing to do in your free time?

Where / quiet / area?

What / bad / thing about this place?

What / quick / way to travel around?

LESSON **18**
Present perfect

Vocabulary Travel: verb + noun combinations
Grammar Present perfect with *yet* and *already*
Language to go Saying what you've done so far

Getting ready

Aim

To practise present perfect and
already/yet

Materials

One copy of the sheet per pair

Time

25 minutes

Preparation

Copy the sheet as above and cut
into Sheets A and B

Procedure

1 Explain to students that they are going to read about two different
   people (a Spanish boy and a German girl) who are going to the US for
   a month to study English. Elicit some ideas for preparations they
   might need to make, e.g. *book a course/arrange somewhere to
   live/buy a dictionary/book tickets*. Pre-teach *to book* and *a guidebook*.
2 Divide the students into As and Bs. Explain that As will read about
   José from Spain and Bs will read about Brigitte from Germany. Hand
   out copies of the texts and give students three minutes to read them.
3 Students now work in pairs (A+B). Ask them to turn over their texts
   and tell their partner what José/Brigitte has/hasn't done yet.
   Elicit one example for José, e.g. *He's already booked his course*.
   Explain that the partner can also ask questions. Elicit one example for
   Brigitte, e.g. *Has she booked her course yet? Yes, she has*.
4 When they have finished, let them look back at their texts to see if
   they have forgotten anything (and tell their partner if they have).
5 Still in pairs, students now write four sentences about José and four
   sentences about Brigitte using the present perfect and *yet/already*.
   Monitor and check for mistakes.
6 Feedback by eliciting some of the sentences round the class and
   writing them on the board.

Extension

Speaking: Ask students to imagine that they are going to a different city
to study and think about what preparations they have made. Then in
pairs, they should ask each other what they have/haven't done yet.

Sheet A

Read about José's preparations for his trip to the US.
What has he already done? What hasn't he done yet?

JOSÉ

Tomorrow José is going to the US to study English
for a month. He's really excited – the course is
booked; he has the address of the flat he's going to
stay in, and his tickets are in his pocket. This
afternoon, he's going to the bank to change some
money and then to the bookshop to buy a Spanish-
English dictionary. Tonight, he's going to meet his
friends in a bar to say goodbye and then pack his
suitcase, not forgetting the new umbrella he
bought yesterday!

Now, without looking at the text, tell Student B what you can remember.

Sheet B

Read about Brigitte's preparations for her trip to the US.
What has she already done? What hasn't she done yet?

BRIGITTE

Brigitte is very nervous about her trip to the US.
She only has one more day and she still needs to
buy her ticket and find somewhere to stay!
After she booked her course, she immediately
went to the shop and bought a guidebook of the
US and a dictionary, but she forgot to change any
money. So, this afternoon she's going to the bank
after the travel agency. Luckily, she packed her
suitcase this morning, so this evening she's going
to have time to say goodbye to her friends.

Now, without looking at the text, tell Student A what you can remember.

Vocabulary Sports, word building
Language focus Past ability with *could* and *be good at*
Language to go Talking about how well you could do things

When they were eighteen ...

Aim

To practise *could / couldn't* and *was / were good at* + adverbs of degree

Materials

One copy of the sheet per pair

Time

25 minutes

Preparation

Copy the sheet as above and cut into Sheets A and B

Procedure

1 Divide students into pairs (A+B) and distribute the sheets accordingly. Explain that they have information about four people when they were eighteen – what they could do and how well. Student A has half the information and Student B has the other half. They have to ask each other questions to complete the missing information. They can refer to the grammar box on page 40 of the Students' Book to help them and to remind them of the symbols used.

2 Elicit a couple of examples, e.g. *Could Frank sing when he was eighteen? Yes, he could sing really well. Was Suzy good at singing? No, she wasn't very good at singing.*

3 While students complete the task, monitor their work and note any mistakes to be corrected later. Watch out for the use of *good at* + noun (not verb) and the position of the adverbs.

4 When they have finished, they can look at each other's sheets to check answers.

5 As feedback, write up any mistakes on the board for correction.

Extension

Writing: Students write a paragraph on what they could do when they were eighteen. For younger groups / students, change this to when they were ten.

When they were eighteen ...

Sheet A

	Frank	Suzy	Richard	Janet
sing		-	+	
dance	- -	+		
play an instrument		*piano* + + +	*drums* + +	
ski		-	+ + +	
speak a foreign language		*German* + +		*French* + +
drive a car			-	+

Sheet B

	Frank	Suzy	Richard	Janet
sing	+ + +			+ +
dance			-	+ + +
play an instrument	*guitar* +			*flute* -
ski		+		- -
speak a foreign language	*French* - -		*Spanish* +	
drive a car	+ +	- -		

Vocabulary Adjectives to describe advertised products
Grammar First conditional (*if* + present simple + *will*)
Language to go Talking about future possibility

Slogan competition

Aim

To practise *if* + present simple + *will* and the vocabulary of advertising

Materials

One sheet per pair

Time

25 minutes

Preparation

Copy the sheet as above

Procedure

1 Ask students if they know what a slogan is and elicit a few famous ones.
2 Divide students into pairs and explain the situation – a local advertising company is having a competition for writing slogans. The best get used in real adverts.
3 Hand out one sheet per pair. Elicit from students what each product is: Sun Flakes, breakfast cereal; Creamy Soft, soap; Red Magic, a soft drink; Futurephone, a mobile phone; Lost Love, a film; Top Speed, a motorbike; Diet chocs, chocolates; First Class, an English-language school.
4 Give each pair a number and ask them to write this number on top of the page. Ask them to look at the first one and elicit some ideas for a slogan.
Possible answers:
Your day will be sunny if you start it with Sun Flakes.
If you feel tired in the morning, Sun Flakes will wake you up.
Then ask students to work in their pairs to write one slogan for each of the other products. Monitor and correct as they are doing this.
5 As feedback, ask students to put their sheets on the walls or pass them around the class. Students should read the sheets and choose the best slogan for each product. At the end, ask them to vote for their favourites and write the most popular on the board.

Extension

Writing: In the same pairs, students choose one of their slogans and design a poster (including their slogan) to advertise it. These can be displayed on the classroom walls.

A local advertising company is running a competition for writing slogans.
The prize is to have one of your slogans used in a new advertisement.
You and your partner decide to enter.

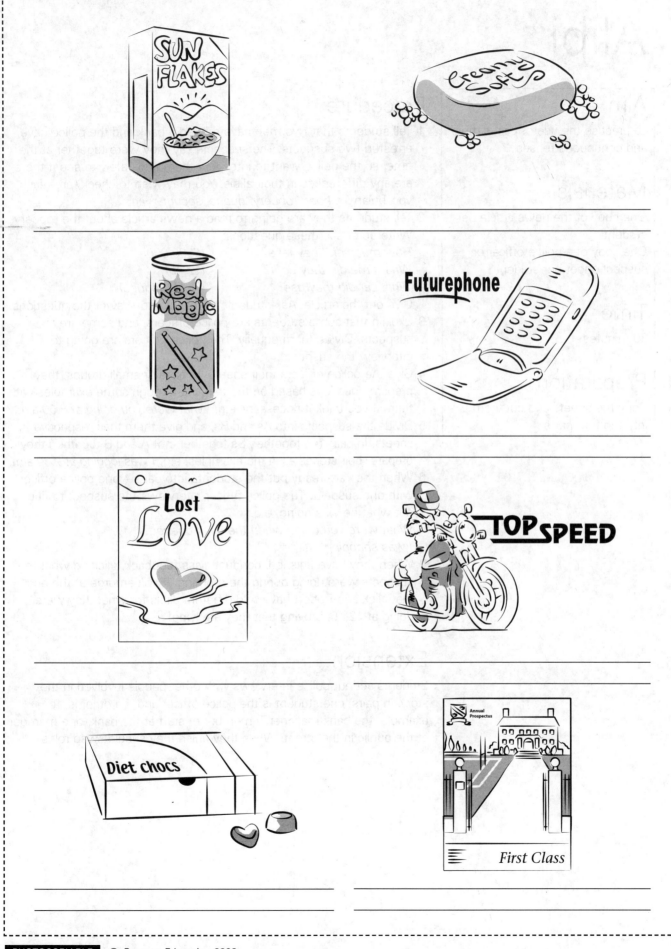

Grammar Past simple and past continuous
Language to go Describing past events in stories

Alibi

Aim

To practise the use of past simple and continuous tenses

Materials

One copy of the news article per student
One copy of a police officer or suspect sheet per student

Time

30 minutes

Preparation

Copy the sheets and cut them into the four parts

Procedure

1 Tell students that two men have robbed a bank and the police have arrested two suspects. The suspects say they were together at the time, so the police want to interview them separately to see if there are any differences in their alibis. You may wish to check/pre-teach vocabulary: *robber*, *robbery*, *queue*, *security van*.

2 Tell students they are going to read a news article about the robbery. Write up or say these questions:

How much did they take?   (£500,000)
What time did they do it?   (12.45)
What car did they use?   (Ford Mondeo)

Give out the article. Ask students to read it and answer the questions.

3 Explain that some students are police officers, and some are suspects. Divide them equally. The police officers are going to interview the suspects.

4 Give the police officers their sheets. In pairs or small groups, they prepare questions based on the text. Go through some examples with them if you think it necessary, e.g. *What were you doing at 8.00 a.m.?*

5 Divide the suspects into As and Bs, and give them their respective sheets. In pairs (As together, Bs together, **not** A and B together) they prepare their stories as in the examples, e.g. *I was jogging at 7.30 a.m.*

6 When they are ready put the students into pairs – one police officer with one suspect. The police officer interviews the suspect to find out what he was doing, e.g.:
What were you doing when the bank opened?
I was shopping.

7 When they have finished, conduct class feedback, eliciting what the suspects were doing during the morning. It will emerge at the end that Nick and Robert have two different alibis for what they were doing at 12.45, proving that they are lying!

Extension

Students act out police interviews with other people involved in the story. In pairs, one student is the police officer and the other is, for example, the bank manager, a member of staff at the bank, or a member of the public in the street. When they finish they should swap roles.

LUNCHTIME BANK ROBBERY IN TOWN CENTRE

Two robbers escaped with £500,000 yesterday lunchtime from the Thrift Bank. Police believe it was a well-planned crime carried out by experienced criminals.

It seemed like a normal day at the bank; manager Mark Countham started work at 8.00, and was making phone calls when the staff arrived at 9.00. There was already a queue when the bank opened for business at 9.30, and it was busy all morning. A security van arrived just before 11.00 with more money. At 12.30, Mr Countham and three of his staff went out for lunch. Exactly fifteen minutes later, at 12.45, two armed robbers ran in to the bank and demanded the money.

They drove away in a red Ford Mondeo. Police are asking anyone who saw anything to call them on 0600 484585.

Police Officer

Write questions to find out what the suspects were doing on the day of the robbery.

What were you doing at ….a.m.?
What were you doing when … ?
Were you …at … p.m.?

Suspect A – Nick Cash

You say that you were with Robert Loot all day. Make notes about what you were doing, from the information below.

I was … at … a.m.
We were … at … p.m.
I was … when the bank ….

7.30	jogging
8.45	home, breakfast
9.20	shopping
10.45	home, watch TV
12.00	lunch
12.40	tennis

Suspect B – Robert Loot

You say that you were with Nick Cash all day. Make notes about what you were doing, from the information below.

I was … at … a.m.
We were … at … p.m.
I was … when the bank ….

7.30	jogging
8.45	home, breakfast
9.20	shopping
10.45	home, watch TV
12.00	lunch
12.40	swimming

 © Pearson Education 2002

LESSON **22**
Verb patterns

Vocabulary   Jobs
Grammar   *Like* + *-ing* and *would like to* + infinitive with *to*
Language to go   Talking about career preferences

Job search

Aim
To practise talking about career preferences using *Do you like* + *-ing* and *Would you like to* + infinitive and vocabulary related to jobs

Materials
One copy of the sheet

Time
25 minutes

Preparation
Copy the sheet and cut it up into separate cards

Procedure
1 Ask students about their experience of looking for work and elicit various ways and places to find a job (contact local companies, newspaper ads, ask family, etc.). Teach *job seeker* (a person looking for a job) and *job centre* (a place that matches job seekers to available jobs).
2 Divide the class in two: half the students will be job seekers and the other half will be people working in job centres.
3 Give each student an appropriate card. If there are fewer than sixteen students, omit one or more of the following pairs: A/3, B/6, C/1, D/2, E/8, F/5, G/4, H/7. If there are more than sixteen students, make an extra copy of one or more of those pairs.
4 Tell students to read their cards and check vocabulary. Ask the job seekers to think about what sort of job would be suitable for them. Ask the job centre people to think about what qualities someone would need to do the jobs on their cards.
5 Spread the 'job centres' around the classroom and explain that the object is for job seekers to find an ideal job and for the job centres to fill their vacant positions.
6 The job seekers should then move about the classroom from centre to centre explaining what they like and what they would like to do. The job-centre students should try to sell one of their jobs, giving all the reasons why the job seeker would be suitable for it. If the seeker disagrees, he/she should explain why and move to another job centre.
7 To keep the activity lively, shout 'change' every few minutes and have all the seekers move on to the next centre.
8 At the end, get feedback from the job seekers on which job they want and why, and from the job centres on which jobs they managed to fill.

SUGGESTED ANSWER KEY
A/3a (English teacher)   B/6a (nurse)   C/1a (office manager)
D/2b (vet)   E/8a (graphic designer)   F/5b (police officer)
G/4b (web designer)   H/7b (airline cabin crew)

22

Job search

Job seeker A	Job seeker B	Job seeker C	Job seeker D
You like: • being creative • meeting people **You'd like to:** • work with children • travel more	**You like:** • working with people • wearing a uniform **You'd like to:** • have responsibility • help people	**You like:** • working in an office • money and economics **You'd like to:** • have responsibility • train people	**You like:** • being with animals • science **You'd like to:** • work outside • earn a good salary

Job seeker E	Job seeker F	Job seeker G	Job seeker H
You like: • being creative • drawing **You'd like to:** • work alone • choose the hours you work	**You like:** • being active • helping people **You'd like to:** • wear a uniform • work outside	**You like:** • working with computers • being artistic **You'd like to:** • earn a lot of money • work from home	**You like:** • working in a team • food and drink **You'd like to:** • travel a lot • meet people

Job centre 1	Job centre 2	Job centre 3	Job centre 4
You have two jobs available: **a) OFFICE MANAGER** (must want to work in an office and help train people) **b) FARMER** (must like animals and working outside)	You have two jobs available: **a) PHOTOGRAPHER** (can choose working hours; good salary) **b) VET** (must like animals; good salary)	You have two jobs available: **a) ENGLISH TEACHER** (must be creative and like working with children) **b) COMPUTER ENGINEER** (must want responsibility and like working with computers)	You have two jobs available: **a) CHEF** (must like food and drink and want to train people) **b) WEB DESIGNER** (must like working with computers; good salary)

Job centre 5	Job centre 6	Job centre 7	Job centre 8
You have two jobs available: **a) JOURNALIST** (can choose working hours; must be creative) **b) POLICE OFFICER** (must be active and like helping people)	You have two jobs available: **a) NURSE** (must want responsibility and to help people) **b) RECEPTIONIST** (must want to help people and work long hours)	You have two jobs available: **a) ADVERTISING EXECUTIVE** (must be creative; good salary) **b) AIRLINE CABIN CREW** (must like working in a team and travelling)	You have two jobs available: **a) GRAPHIC DESIGNER** (must like drawing and be happy working alone) **b) SKI INSTRUCTOR** (must be good with people and like working outside)

Vocabulary   Materials and possessions
Grammar   Present simple passive
Language to go   Describing the origins of products

Great inventions

Aim

To practise describing products using the passive (present simple and infinitive) and materials vocabulary (metal, glass, plastic, leather, cotton)

Materials

One copy of Sheets A, B and C per group of three students

Time

25 minutes

Preparation

Copy and cut Sheets A, B and C as above

Procedure

1 Ask students to think of the greatest invention ever and compare opinions.
2 Now ask them to think of a clever but simple invention (e.g. a zip) but not to say what it is.
3 They now have to describe it to the class without naming it. Give an example first and highlight the structures (e.g. *It is made of cotton and metal, it can be used to keep your coat or pocket closed*).
4 Divide the class into pairs and give each pair a copy each of Sheet A, B or C, so both students in the pair are looking at the same invention.
5 Students work together to complete the text, deciding if the verbs should be active or passive. Help with vocabulary if necessary.
6 Students reform into threes (A+B+C). Students fold their piece of paper between the picture and text and then, showing the picture to the others, describe it, trying to remember as much of the text as possible.

Extension

Speaking: Repeat steps 2 and 3 above, as they should now be more confident with the structures.

Writing: With more creative students, get them to think of other strange inventions to draw and describe. Get them to think about what simple object would make their lives easier. If necessary, give them suggestions, for example:

• 'waterproof newspaper covers': you slip one page of the newspaper into each cover and can then read the paper in the bath without any problems;
• 'finger-mounted toothbrushes': ideal for travellers, it's like a small, one-fingered glove with a brush attached.

ANSWER KEY
Sheet A
is made; wear; move; be put on; take
Sheet B
is made; be used; be seen; use; get
Sheet C
is made; be worn; travel; like; be removed

23

Great inventions

Sheet A

Do you often need your key when your hands are full? Yes? Then you need a HEADBAND KEYRING. This clever idea *makes / is made* of leather and plastic. You just *wear / are worn* it on your head and *move / are moved* your head to the door. Remember, it must *put on / be put on* when your hands are free, <u>before</u> you *take / is taken* your shopping from the car.

Sheet B

Do you find it difficult to see things on high shelves and cupboards? Yes? Then you need a MIRROR FOR DIFFICULT PLACES. The mirror *makes / is made* of metal and glass, and it can *use / be used* in any room in the house. All those objects on high shelves can *see / be seen* easily, and you can also *use / be used* it to look under cupboards. Unfortunately, it cannot *get / be got* the objects for you.

Sheet C

Do you want to have more space on trains? Then you need a PERSONAL SPACE PROTECTOR. It *makes / is made* of metal and cotton and can *wear / be worn* when you *travel / are travelled* on a train. But be careful – other passengers may not *like / be liked* it. And the protector should always *remove / be removed* before you go through a door.

© *Pearson Education 2002*

Vocabulary   The theatre
Grammar   *A / an* and *the*
Language to go   Talking about a theatre show

On with the show!

Aim

To practise use of articles and to talk about the theatre and cinema

Materials

One copy of the board game and one dice per group of three or four students and a counter for each player

Time

25 minutes

Preparation

Copy the board game as above (enlarge it to A3 if possible)

Procedure

1 Divide the class into groups of three or four students.
2 Pre-teach vocabulary where necessary (e.g. *interval*, *stalls* (in front of the stage), *circle* (upstairs)).
3 Students take it in turns to roll the dice and move around the board. If a dice is not available, use a coin and move one square for heads and three squares for tails.
4 When a student lands on a square, the person on his / her left must ask the question, thinking about which article (*a*, *an*, *the* or no article) to use in the blanks.
5 The student who rolled the dice answers the question. Encourage others to ask follow-up questions and to respond to what their colleagues are saying.
6 If students finish too quickly, they can go back to the start. If someone lands on a square that they have answered previously they should move to the next square.

Extension

Writing: Students choose one of the questions and write an answer to it.

ANSWER KEY

1 Which do you prefer, **the** theatre or **the** cinema? (*genres*)
2 Talk about **a** film you've seen recently. (*any film*) What was **the** best part? (*superlative*)
3 What's **the** best film you've ever seen? (*superlative*)
4 Which is better, going to **the** cinema or watching **a** video? (*cinema as a genre, any video*)
5 Do you prefer to sit in **the** stalls or in **the** circle? (*only ones in theatre*)
6 Do you like musicals? (*in general*)
7 Have you ever seen **a** musical by Andrew Lloyd Webber? (*one of the musicals he wrote*)
8 What do you think films will be like in **the** future? (*films in general, only one future*)
9 Talk about **a** film that made you cry. (*any film*) What was **the** story? (*only story in that film*)

10 Which is better, **the** film or **the** book? (*only ones made / written about that story*)
11 When was **the** last time that you went to **the** theatre? (*specific time, genre*)
12 Have you ever acted in **a** play? (*any play*)
13 What do you do during **the** interval? (*usually only one interval*)
14 Talk about **a** film that you didn't like. (*any film*)
15 What did you eat during **the** last film that you saw? (*specific film you have gone to see*)
16 Where do you like to sit, at **the** front or at **the** back? (*specific places*)
17 Talk about **an** actor or actress you would like to meet. (*any actor / actress: compare with 'the actor you would most like to meet'*)

24

On with the show!

START

1 — May 23
Which do you prefer, ___ theatre or ___ cinema?
One Adult — 7:30 pm

2 — May 23
Talk about ___ film you've seen recently. What was ___ best part?
One Adult — 7:30 pm

5 — May 23
Do you prefer to sit in ___ stalls or in ___ circle?
One Adult — 7:30 pm

4 — May 23
Which is better; going to ___ cinema or watching ___ video?
One Adult — 7:30 pm

3 — May 23
What's ___ best film you've ever seen?
One Adult — 7:30 pm

6 — May 23
Do you like ___ musicals?
One Adult — 7:30 pm

7 — May 23
Have you ever seen ___ musical by Andrew Lloyd Webber? Which?
One Adult — 7:30 pm

8 — May 23
What do you think ___ films will be like in ___ future?
One Adult — 7:30 pm

11 — May 23
When was ___ last time that you went to ___ theatre?
One Adult — 7:30 pm

10 — May 23
Which is better, ___ film or ___ book?
One Adult — 7:30 pm

9 — May 23
Talk about ___ film that made you cry. What was ___ story?
One Adult — 7:30 pm

12 — May 23
Have you ever acted in ___ play? Would you like to?
One Adult — 7:30 pm

13 — May 23
What do you do during ___ interval?
One Adult — 7:30 pm

14 — May 23
Talk about ___ film that you didn't like.
One Adult — 7:30 pm

FINISH

17 — May 23
Talk about ___ actor or actress you would like to meet.
One Adult — 7:30 pm

16 — May 23
Where do you like to sit, at ___ front or at ___ back?
One Adult — 7:30 pm

15 — May 23
What did you eat during ___ last film that you saw?
One Adult — 7:30 pm

Vocabulary Verb + noun combinations
Grammar *Have to, don't have to, mustn't*
Language to go Expressing obligation and prohibition

You have to do this!

Aim

To practise language for expressing obligation and prohibition

Materials

One copy of Sheets A and B per pair of students

Time

25 minutes

Preparation

Copy and cut Sheets A and B as above

Procedure

1 Ask the class if they think learning English is easy or difficult. Ask them how they feel about learning vocabulary and to compare speaking, listening, reading and writing. Ask for suggestions for ways of making learning easier, such as lots of practice, organisation and good reference materials.
2 Tell the class that they are going to write some rules for what makes a good student.
3 Divide the class into groups of two or three.
4 Give half the groups Sheet A (what students need to do during a course) and the other half Sheet B (what students need to do after the course has finished). Sheet B is probably slightly harder, so would be better with stronger pairs.
5 Students work together to write five rules. Monitor and correct within each group as necessary.
6 Reorganise students into A+B pairs. They take it in turns to read out their suggestions and discuss them.
7 As a class, discuss the best rules.

Extension

Speaking: Discuss what 'a good dictionary' is and show examples.
Do the same for 'a good grammar book' and 'a good book for learning vocabulary'.

SUGGESTED ANSWER KEY

A
• You have to have a good dictionary.
• You have to do your homework.
• You don't have to be correct all the time.
• You mustn't be late.
• You have to have a good vocabulary book to keep new words in.
• You mustn't sleep in class.

B
• You mustn't give up!
• You have to practise a little every day.
• You have to revise your notes.
• You have to watch some English-language TV or listen to English-language radio.
• You have to find someone to practise speaking with.
• You have to go to an English-speaking country.

Sheet A

Think about what you need to do during your course to be successful at learning English.
Write five rules beginning *You must / mustn't / have to / don't have to ...*

1 _____
_____

2 _____
_____

3 _____
_____

4 _____
_____

5 _____
_____

Sheet B

Think about what you need to do after your course to be successful at learning English.
Write five rules beginning *You must / mustn't / have to / don't have to ...*

1 _____
_____

2 _____
_____

3 _____
_____

4 _____
_____

5 _____
_____

Vocabulary Food
Grammar The future with *going to* and *will*
Language to go Planned and spontaneous decisions

Party plans

Aim

To practise *will* and *going to* (spontaneous vs. planned decisions)

Materials

One copy of the sheet per pair of students

Time

25 minutes

Preparation

Copy the sheet as above
Cut each one into sets of twelve question cards and place each set in order in a pile face down with Question 1 on top

Procedure

1 Divide the class into pairs.
2 In each pair, students imagine that one of them (Student A) is about to have a birthday and has decided to have a party. Now he/she needs to decide on some details and has to plan it all with the help of his/her partner (Student B). If you have an odd number, have one group of three with one Student A and two Student Bs deciding together.
3 Tell students that there are twelve questions on the cards and that Student A should try to answer as many as possible in a reasonable time limit (five to ten minutes). Student B must ask the questions and has to try and remember the answers.
4 Student B quickly asks the questions one by one, encouraging Student A to give quick, spontaneous answers to each, which Student B tries to remember before going on to the next question.
5 After the time is up, Student Bs summarise to a larger group or the rest of the class what their partners are going to do.
6 Students vote on which party they will go to and why (e.g. *I'll go to Juan's because he's going to play my favourite music.*).

Extension

Speaking: Find out if any students are really planning to have a party or are going to have one in the near future.

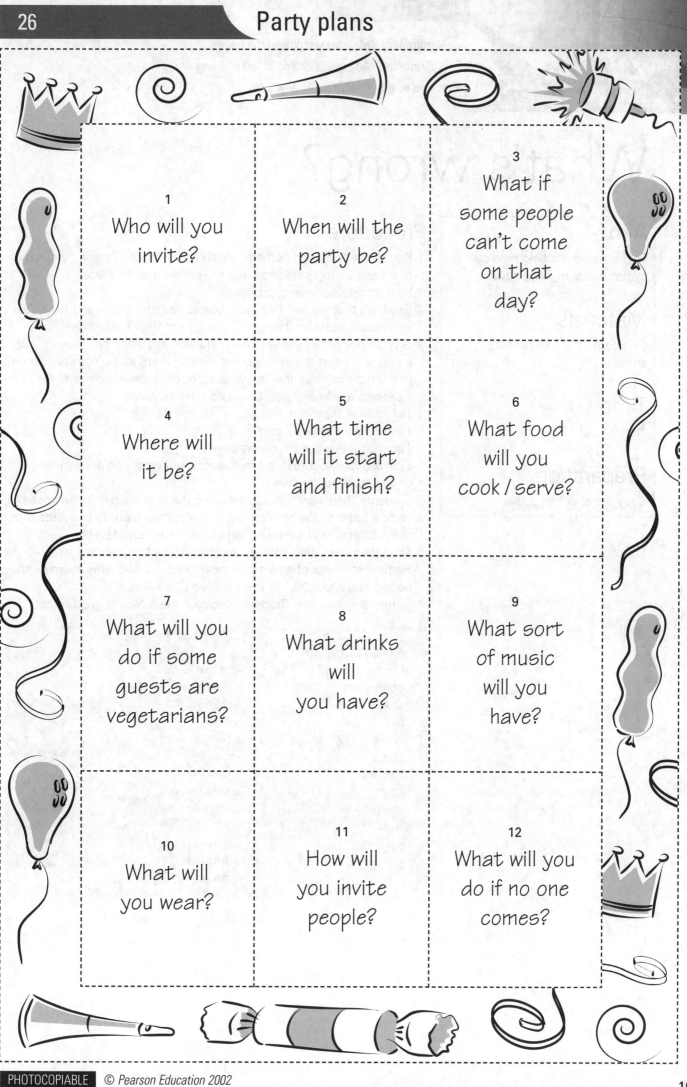

1
Who will you invite?

2
When will the party be?

3
What if some people can't come on that day?

4
Where will it be?

5
What time will it start and finish?

6
What food will you cook / serve?

7
What will you do if some guests are vegetarians?

8
What drinks will you have?

9
What sort of music will you have?

10
What will you wear?

11
How will you invite people?

12
What will you do if no one comes?

Vocabulary Medical symptoms: the body
Grammar Adjectives ending in -ed and -ing
Language to go Describing how you feel

What's wrong?

Aim

To practise describing medical symptoms and giving advice

Materials

One copy of the sheet per student

Time

30 minutes

Preparation

Copy the sheet as above

Procedure

1 Revise the following items of vocabulary from the lesson by miming them and asking students what the problem is: *headache, sore throat, depressed, worried.*
2 Establish that we say *I've got a headache/sore throat* and *I am/feel depressed* and why (*I've got* + noun, *I am/feel* + adjective).
3 Give a copy of the sheet to each student and ask them to work with a partner to sort the expressions, writing them in the correct column. In the right column, they must also decide if the word needs the indefinite article *a* or not. Compare the following:
I am sick + I feel sick
I am cold + I've got a cold
I am hot + I've got a temperature
I am allergic (adj.) *to* (not *I feel allergic*) + *I've got an allergy* (n.)
4 Check students' answers.
5 Students then work individually using the expressions in the boxes to write a letter to the problem page. Encourage them to give details of the problem, how/when it started and how they feel about it.
6 They then pass their letter to another student who writes a reply. Remind students of structures they could use and write them on the board: *You should … / If you do X, you'll be fine.*
7 Return the answers. Students decide if the advice is good or not.

ANSWER KEY	
I am … / I feel …	**I've got …**
depressed	a headache
sick	a rash
hot	a cold
weak	a temperature
tired	spots
worried	a pain in my …
cold	a sore throat
allergic to	a stomach ache
faint	flu
	hay fever
	diarrhoea
	a cough

- Sort the words / phrases from the box into the correct column.
  One can go in both columns, but there is a difference in meaning.

> headache   rash   sick   spots   temperature   sore throat   stomachache
> cold   tired   hay fever   depressed   cough   faint   pain in my ...   flu
> worried   hot   diarrhoea   allergic to   weak   allergy

I am ... / I feel ...	I've got (a) ...
depressed	a headache
worried	a sore throat

- Write to a magazine and explain your health problem. Say what the problem is, how you feel, when it started and ask for some advice.

  Dear Dr Marion,
  I am a little bit worried because I ...

- Read the letter you are given and write a reply with a suggestion.

  Dear ...
  It sounds as if you ...

  © *Pearson Education 2002*

Vocabulary Furniture and fittings
Grammar Present perfect to describe present result
Language to go Talking about changes you can see

All change!

Aim

To practise talking about changes using the present perfect and vocabulary of furniture

Materials

One copy of the sheet per student

Time

25 minutes

Preparation

Copy the sheet as above

Procedure

1 Hand out a copy of the sheet to each student.
2 Ask them to look at the top plan, identify the various items of furniture and say where they are (e.g. *it's in the corner, next to, between,* etc.) to revise the prepositions of place.
3 Ask them to look at the plan again and think about whether they like the design or not.
4 Tell them to imagine that they have just rented this room and want to make it more personal. They have enough time and money to make any changes they want. Elicit verbs to describe the changes that they could make (e.g. *move, remove, replace, paint, change, cover, polish, put up, re-cover*) and write them up on the board.
5 They now have ten minutes to redesign the room, get it the way they want it and draw the layout on the bottom floor plan.
6 They then compare their plan with that of their partner and explain what they have done and why.

Extension

Speaking: Get students to discuss what changes they would like to make to the classroom.

BEFORE
Look at the plan of the room below.

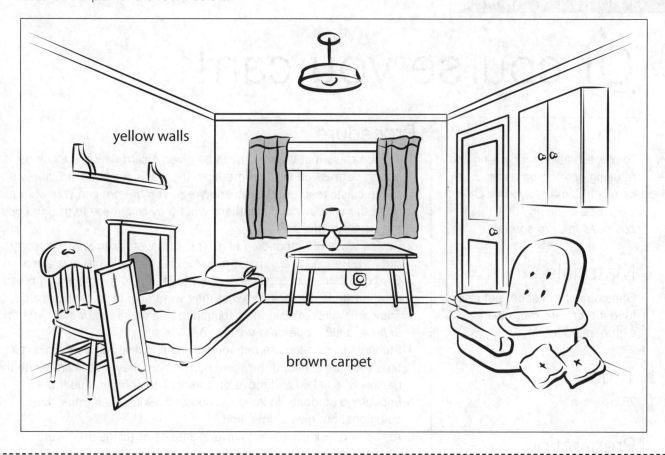

yellow walls

brown carpet

AFTER
Now redesign the room how you would like it.

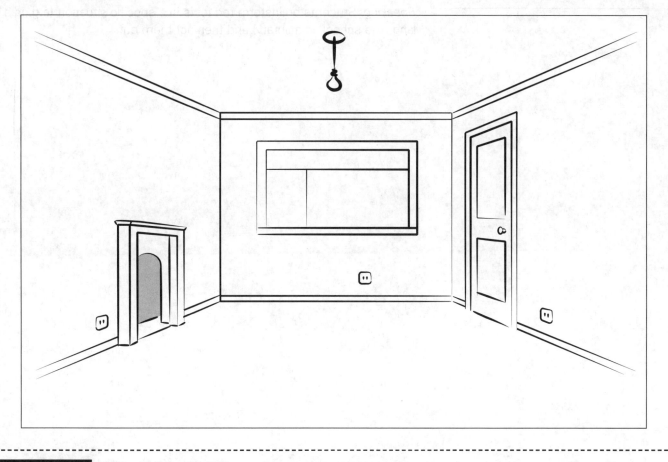

Of course you can!

Aim

To practise asking for, giving and refusing permission using *can/could/may I ... , is it OK if I ...?* , *Yes, certainly/of course/sure, I'm sorry (but ...)*

Materials

One copy of the sheet per class (two if there are more than eighteen students)

Time

25 minutes

Preparation

Copy the sheet onto card if possible and cut it up into eighteen separate cue cards

Procedure

1 Tell the class that they will each be given a card which is a cue for asking permission to do something. If there is a spare card, show it to the class, read out the situation (e.g. *you are hot and you want to open the window*) and ask them what they might say (e.g. *Can I open the window, please?*).

2 Revise ways of responding (e.g. *Yes, of course/certainly; I'm sorry, but ... *). Remind them that if they refuse, it is polite to give a reason.

3 Give one card to each student, then tell them to mingle and approach another student to ask for what they want according to their card. They must first explain the situation (e.g. *Excuse me, it's very warm in here, could I open the window?*).

4 Students must alternate between giving and refusing permission each time they are asked. If they give permission, they swap cards with the person who asked and move off to speak to another student.

5 Encourage students to keep moving and asking each other the questions, but give a time limit.

6 At the end, ask the class to give examples of things they were allowed and not allowed to do.

Extension

Speaking: Students brainstorm requests in a specific situation (e.g. in a language school, in a library) and then act them out.

You are hot and you want to open the window.

You are in a friend's house and you want to use the toilet.

You are in a bar and you want to take an unused chair.

You are cold and you want to close the window.

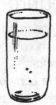

You are in a classroom and you want to go out for a drink of water.

You want to borrow a book from someone.

You are in a fast-food restaurant and you want to sit in a seat next to another person.

You are in a restaurant and you want to smoke a cigar.

You want to use another person's mobile phone.

You feel ill and you want to go home.

You are in a dark room and you want to put a light on.

You are on a train and you want to read another person's paper.

You want to arrive late tomorrow because you have a dentist's appointment.

You want to have the day off tomorrow.

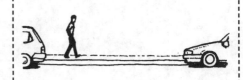

You want to park somewhere.

You are in a restaurant and you want to change tables.

You want to leave your suitcase in a shop.

You want to use another person's umbrella.

LESSON **30**
Conditionals

Vocabulary   Verbs and their opposites
Grammar   *Would* + infinitive (without *to*)
Language to go   Talking about imaginary situations

Would you really?

Aim

To practise talking about imaginary situations using *would* and *wouldn't*

Materials

One copy of the board game and a coin per group of four students and a counter for each player

Time

30 minutes

Preparation

Copy the board game as above (enlarge it to A3 if possible)

Procedure

1 Divide the class into groups of about four.
2 Pre-teach vocabulary where necessary (e.g. *boss*, *classmate*, *naked*, *experience*).
3 Give one copy of the game to each group and ask them to think about the questions. Tell them that they are going to play the game by moving round the board, answering the questions as they land on them.
4 Establish that if a student lands on a square marked 'Group question', someone else in the group can ask a question. Give them a few minutes to think of questions that they would like to ask others in their group. Get them to write down a few questions individually.
5 Students take it in turns to move by tossing a coin: they move one square for heads and three squares for tails, answering the question that they land on.
6 As students play the game, encourage them to respond to what their colleagues are saying.
7 When a player lands on a 'Group question', the others in the group decide which of their prepared questions to ask.
8 If one group finishes earlier than the others, they can discuss questions that didn't come up, either on the board or from those they prepared.

Extension

Speaking: Ask students to tell the whole class the most interesting / unbelievable / surprising answer that they heard.

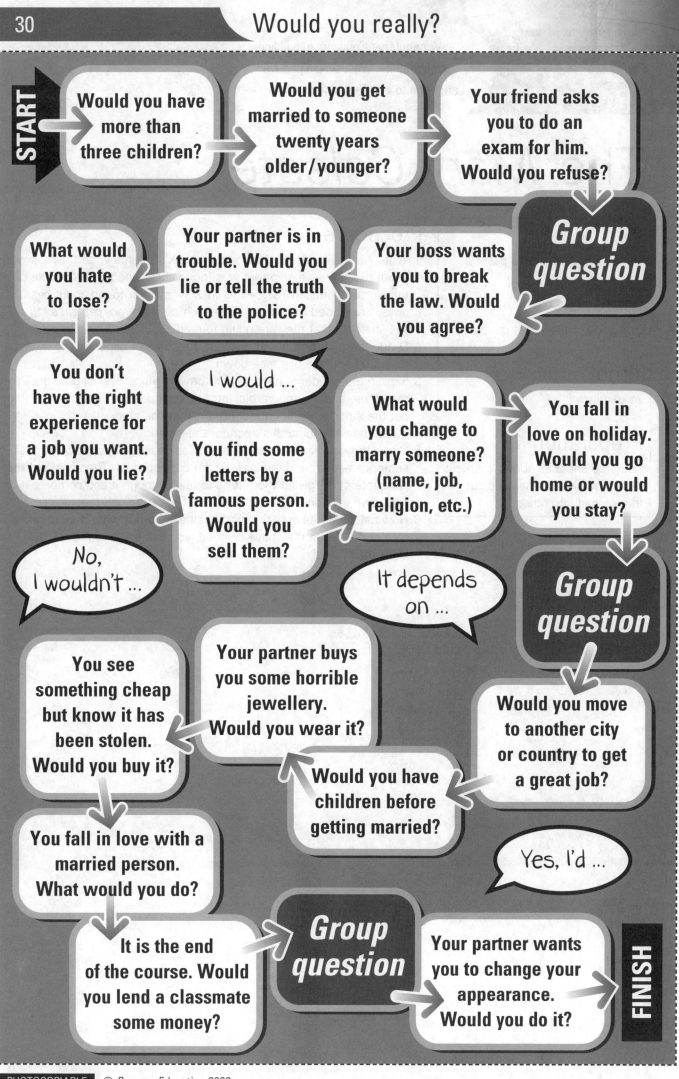

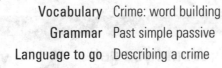

Vocabulary   Crime: word building
Grammar   Past simple passive
Language to go   Describing a crime

The *Mary Celeste*

Aim

To practise past simple passive

Materials

One copy of the sheet per pair

Time

25 minutes

Preparation

Copy the sheet as above, then cut each worksheet in half and cut the top half into strips

Procedure

1 Write *Mary Celeste* on the board and ask students what they know about this (it was a ship that was found abandoned in the middle of the North Atlantic in 1872 – the crew was never found and it has always remained a mystery). Pre-teach *crew*, *cargo*, *captain's log*.

2 Tell students that they are going to read about the *Mary Celeste*. Divide them into pairs and give out the strips of paper – they must be mixed up and in a pile face down.

3 Explain that students have to first turn the strips over one by one, read them and put the verb(s) into the past passive. They should then put the strips into the correct order to tell the story.

4 While they are doing this, monitor their work.

5 When they are finished, as feedback, ask each pair to read out one sentence each round the class in the correct order. Then give out the complete story, giving them time to read through it and compare it to their own version.

6 Now ask students in their pairs to tell each other what they think happened. When they have finished, you can ask them to tell the class their ideas.

The *Mary Celeste* _____ (build) in Nova Scotia in 1860. Originally, the ship _____ (call) *Amazon*.

Ten years later, in 1870, she _____ (buy) in New York for $3,000 and she _____ (rename) *Mary Celeste*. The new captain of the ship was Benjamin Briggs.

On 7 November 1872, a cargo of alcohol _____ (put) on the ship, and the *Mary Celeste* left New York for Genoa, Italy. Captain Briggs, his wife, young daughter and a crew of eight were on board – they _____ (never see) again.

On 4 December 1872, a ship _____ (see) by the crew of the *Dei Grata* in the North Atlantic. When they got closer, they saw that it was the *Mary Celeste*.

There was nobody on board. The lifeboat and some of the alcohol were missing. The ship's papers were gone, but the captain's log _____ (find).

The last written entry was 25 November, nine days before the ship _____ (discover). The ship was in perfect order, and there was no sign of violence or a reason to leave.

In fact, on the table in the kitchen, dinner _____ (find), ready to be eaten. There was also enough food and water for six months. What happened to the crew?

_____ they _____ (murder)? _____ they _____ (take) by aliens? A lot of stories _____ (tell) about the mystery.

A story about a ship called the *Marie Celeste* _____ even _____ (write) by the famous writer Sir Arthur Conan Doyle. Nobody knows the real story – what do you think happened?

The mystery of the *Mary Celeste*

The *Mary Celeste* **was built** in Nova Scotia in 1860. Originally the ship **was called** *Amazon*. Ten years later, in 1870, she **was bought** in New York for $3,000 and she **was renamed** *Mary Celeste*. The new captain of the ship was Benjamin Briggs. On 7 November 1872, a cargo of alcohol **was put** on the ship, and the *Mary Celeste* left New York for Genoa, Italy. Captain Briggs, his wife, young daughter and a crew of eight were on board – they **were never seen** again. On 4 December 1872, a ship **was seen** by the crew of the *Dei Grata* in the North Atlantic. When they got closer, they saw that it was the *Mary Celeste*. There was nobody on board. The lifeboat and some of the alcohol was missing. The ship's papers were gone, but the captain's log **was found**. The last written entry was 25 November, nine days before the ship **was discovered**. The ship was in perfect order and there was no sign of violence or a reason to leave. In fact, on the table in the kitchen, dinner **was found**, ready to be eaten. There was also enough food and water for six months. What happened to the crew? **Were they murdered?** **Were they taken** by aliens? A lot of stories **were told** about the mystery. A story about a ship called the *Mary Celeste* **was even written** by the famous writer Sir Arthur Conan Doyle. Nobody knows the real story – what do you think happened?

Vocabulary Phrasal verbs
Grammar Verbs with *-ing* form / infinitive (with *to*)
Language to go Talking about changing habits

True or false?

Aim

To practise verbs + infinitive / *-ing* forms and two-part verbs

Materials

One copy of the sheet per group of four students

Time

25–30 minutes

Preparation

Copy the sheets as above and cut them into twelve squares

Procedure

1 Divide students into groups of four (A, B, C and D in each group, but different groups from the ones in Exercise 5 in the Students' Book). On the board, write three sentences about yourself using one of the verbs on the sheet, one true and two false, e.g.
   A: *I gave up smoking ten years ago.*
   B: *I've given up beer.*
   C: *I gave up chocolate last week.*

2 Ask students in their groups to discuss which they think is the correct answer, giving reasons. As feedback, ask each group for their conclusion and give them the correct answer.

3 Now give out one set of twelve cards per group. Ask students to take three cards each. Explain that for each verb, they should write three sentences, one true and two false, as you did in the example.

4 When they have finished, Student A should read out his / her first three sentences to the rest of the group. The group should then discuss together which one they think is true. When they have decided, Student A tells them the answer. Student B now does the same, then Student C and Student D. This continues around the group until they have all read out the sentences for their three verbs.

5 As feedback, ask around the class if anyone found out anything interesting or surprising about their classmates.

try	decide	begin
cut down on	want	carry on
give up	need	would like
take up	stop	start

Vocabulary   Regular activities: verb + noun combinations
Grammar   Subject and non-subject questions, present simple
Language to go   Asking questions

The bouncer

Aim

To practise subject and non-subject questions

Materials

One copy of the sheet per pair

Time

25 minutes

Preparation

Copy the sheet as above and cut into Sheets A and B

Procedure

1 Ask students if they know what a *bouncer* is. If nobody knows, ask them what a *doorman* is. Establish what a bouncer does in his/her job, i.e. stands at the door of a nightclub/bar, stops some people going in, helps if there is a problem/fight. Pre-teach *day off* – you could ask students what they think a bouncer does on his/her day off.

2 Divide the class into two and designate one half A and the other half B. Explain that they are going to read about a bouncer, but that the two halves will have different information. They will need to ask questions to complete all the information.

3 Give out the texts and ask them to work in pairs (A+A, B+B). They should look at the gaps in their text and write the necessary questions. Do the first two gaps as examples.
(1) _____ is his day off? ➔ _____*When*_____ is his day off?
(2) _____ wakes him up? ➔ _____*Who*_____ wakes him up?

4 While the pairs write their questions, monitor and correct their work if necessary.

5 Now have them work in different pairs (A+B). Students need to ask each other the questions to complete the text.

6 As feedback, ask students if any of them would like to work as a bouncer. Why/Why not?

7 Ask students to compare their texts and check their answers.

ANSWER KEY

John is a bouncer at the Roxy nightclub in Manchester. He works six days a week, and (1) _____*Monday*_____ is his day off. His day begins at two o'clock in the afternoon, when (2) _____*his mum*_____ wakes him up. After a breakfast of eggs, bacon and sausages, (3) _____*John*_____ does the shopping in the local supermarket, and in the afternoon he makes a few phone calls to his friends and sometimes goes to (4) _____*the pub*_____ for a beer. He starts work at nine p.m. and usually finishes at (5) _____*four a.m.*_____ . Sometimes he works alone, but usually (6) _*one of his friends*_ works with him. He meets (7) _*a lot of interesting and famous people*_ in his job – last week, (8) _____*Madonna*_____ came to the club! After work, they have a drink in (9) _____*the club*_____ , and he goes to bed at about six o'clock. On his day off, his girlfriend comes round to his house and they (10) _____*watch TV*_____ or sometimes go to the cinema. He really enjoys his job, but (11) _*his girlfriend*_ wants to spend more time with him, and (12) _____*his mum*_____ worries about him – she would prefer him to work in an office.

Sheet A

A day in the life of a bouncer

John is a bouncer at the Roxy nightclub in Manchester. He works six days a week, and (1) _____ is his day off. His day begins at two o'clock in the afternoon, when his mum wakes him up. After a breakfast of eggs, bacon and sausages, (3) _____ does the shopping in the local supermarket, and in the afternoon he makes a few phone calls to his friends and sometimes goes to the pub for a beer. He starts work at nine p.m. and usually finishes at (5) _____ . Sometimes he works alone, but usually one of his friends works with him. He meets (7) _____ in his job – last week, Madonna came to the club! After work, they have a drink in (9) _____ , and he goes to bed at about six o'clock. On his day off, his girlfriend comes round to his house and they watch TV or sometimes go to the cinema. He really enjoys his job, but (11) _____ wants to spend more time with him, and his mum worries about him – she would prefer him to work in an office.

Sheet B

A day in the life of a bouncer

John is a bouncer at the Roxy nightclub in Manchester. He works six days a week, and Monday is his day off. His day begins at two o'clock in the afternoon when (2) _____ wakes him up. After a breakfast of eggs, bacon and sausages, John does the shopping in the local supermarket, and in the afternoon he makes a few phone calls to his friends and sometimes goes to (4) _____ . He starts work at nine p.m. and usually finishes at four a.m. Sometimes he works alone, but usually (6) _____ works with him. He meets a lot of interesting and famous people in his job – last week (8) _____ came to the club! After work, they have a drink in the club, and he goes to bed at about six o'clock. On his day off, his girlfriend comes round to his house and they (10) _____ or sometimes go to the cinema. He really enjoys his job, but his girlfriend wants to spend more time with him and (12) _____ worries about him – she would prefer him to work in an office.

Vocabulary Technical equipment
Grammar Relative clauses with *which, that, who* and *where*
Language to go Describing people, places and things

Hi-tech

Aim

To practise vocabulary of technical equipment and to introduce stress patterns for compound nouns

Materials

One copy of the sheet per group of four

Time

30 minutes

Preparation

Copy the sheet onto card as above and cut each one into two sets of twelve cards

Procedure

1 Divide students into groups of four and into two teams within each group.
2 Hand out a set of 24 cards to each group. Students should place them face down on a surface with the small cards and big cards separate. Make sure students don't look at the cards.
3 Explain that this is a memory game. The small cards have nouns on and the big cards have definitions – they need to match them. Use one group to illustrate. Ask one team to turn over a small card and read what it says, e.g. *laptop*. Now ask them to turn over any big card, add the correct relative pronoun and read it out. If the pronoun is correct and they match, the team keeps the two cards and has another go. If not, they turn the cards back over and the next team has a go. The winners are the team with the most cards at the end.
4 While students play the game, monitor their work, but don't answer too many questions about vocabulary (only if it is a word from the definition).
5 As feedback, ask students round the class to read out the nouns and definitions, check answers and clarify any meaning if necessary. As they do this, write the nouns on the board and ask them to mark the stress. All these compound words are stressed on the first syllable except *computer **prog**rammer, **dot.com** millionaire*. Get the class to practise the pronunciation as a whole.
6 Back in their groups, they should take it in turns to read out one of the definitions and the others should say the noun. While they do this, monitor and check for mistakes and the correct stress patterns.

Alternative

As part of step 2, ask students round the class to read out the nouns on the small cards. As they do this, write the nouns on the board and ask them to mark the stress. Get the class to practise the pronunciation as a whole. Don't give any help on meanings at this stage. If you follow this procedure, miss out the pronunciation part of step 5.

Extension

Writing: In pairs, students write definitions of other words connected to technology and then read them out for another pair to guess the words.

screensaver	website	cameraman
palmtop	computer programmer	webcam
dot.com millionaire	laptop	darkroom
cybercafé	web designer	chatroom
Something _____ you can see on your computer screen.	A place _____ you can shop or look for information on a computer.	A person _____ uses a camera to record films, videos or television programmes.
A computer _____ is small enough to put in your pocket.	A person _____ writes programs for computers.	A camera _____ you use with your computer.
A person _____ has made a lot of money from the Internet.	A computer _____ you can take to different places in a bag.	A place _____ traditional photographs are developed.
A place _____ people can use computers and send e-mails.	A person _____ designs material for the Internet.	A place _____ you can meet people on the Internet.

Vocabulary   Sounds people make
Grammar   Present deduction with *must be, might be, can't be*
Language to go   Making deductions

Where am I?

Aim

To practise *might be, can't be, must be, it's, it isn't* for present deduction

Materials

One copy of the sheet per group of four students

Time

30 minutes

Preparation

Copy the sheet as above and cut it into sentences, keeping the different letters together and in the correct order (see also Alternatives)

Procedure

1 Explain that you are going to describe a place in five sentences and they have to guess where the place is. On the board, write:
   Some people are standing and some are sitting down.
   Ask students to make deductions about where the place is, e.g.
   It could be a bus / It might be a party.
2 Write the following sentences on the board, each time asking students to make deductions:
   It is dark outside. (It must be at night.)
   There is loud music. (It can't be a bus – it might be a party or a bar.)
   The barman is serving drinks. (It must be a bar or a nightclub.)
   At 11 o'clock, the barman stops serving drinks. (It must be / It's a pub.)
3 Divide the class into groups of four and divide each group of four into A, B, C and D. Hand out the appropriate sentences to each student so that they get a set of five each – the sentences must be arranged so that when students put them face down on the table, they turn them over in the correct order.
4 Explain that Student A needs to turn over and read out the first card – ask them to do this to illustrate. Then elicit some deductions.
   Tell Student A to continue doing this, each time stopping so the group can make deductions until they have guessed the place.
   Then Student B should do the same with his / her sentences, then Student C and then Student D. Monitor to check they are using the language correctly.
5 When they have finished, as feedback, ask what the four places were.
6 Now divide each group into two pairs. Each pair should think of a place and then write five clues to describe it, getting progressively easier, as in the previous task. Monitor and help if necessary.
7 Now the pairs read out the clues one by one to the other pair in the group so that they can guess the place.

Alternatives

A Cut the sheet into two sections (A and B) instead of twenty individual sentences. Give each student in each group one section and ask them to cover it with another piece of paper. The procedure is as above, except students uncover one sentence at a time instead of turning over the cards.

OR

B Just have one copy of the sheet and read out one sentence at a time, giving the groups time to discuss their deductions. Do Steps 6 and 7 as above.

ANSWER KEY

A On a plane.	C At a concert.
B At a train station.	D In a restaurant.

A1 Someone is snoring.	**B1** There are people waiting.
A2 You can't smoke.	**B2** All the people want to go somewhere.
A3 Some people are nervous.	**B3** You need to buy a ticket.
A4 Everyone is travelling somewhere.	**B4** There are timetables on the wall.
A5 The flight attendant is giving people food and drink.	**B5** There is a train arriving.
C1 There are thousands of people.	**D1** There are people sitting at tables.
C2 The people are in a stadium.	**D2** There is music and the people are talking to each other.
C3 They are clapping and cheering.	**D3** There are flowers on the tables.
C4 Everyone is listening to music.	**D4** Most people are eating.
C5 A group of musicians is playing the music.	**D5** The waiter is bringing food to the customers.

Vocabulary Time expressions with *in, on, at* or no preposition
Grammar Present continuous for future time
Language to go Talking about future arrangements

Pop stars

Aim

To practise present continuous for talking about future plans and *at/on/in* + expressions of time

Materials

One sheet per pair

Time

25 minutes

Preparation

Copy the sheet as above and cut into Sheets A and B

Procedure

1 Elicit the meaning of *boy band* (= a pop group composed of three or more young men).
2 Ask students to choose a name for a new boy band in their country (or in the UK, depending on where they are studying). Tell them that this new boy band wants to become famous in the USA, so they are going on a publicity tour to promote their new album. Elicit what a band might do on a publicity tour, e.g. *meet fans, sign autographs*. Pre-teach *give an interview, appear on TV, play a concert, perform at a club*.
3 Divide the class into pairs (A+B). Explain that you are going to give them the schedule for the five-day tour of the USA which the band are going to do next week. Student A has the first version of the schedule that was planned. Since then, the manager has made some changes, and Student B has the final version. They have to ask each other questions and see how many differences they can find.
4 Hand out the Sheets A and B as appropriate. Students can write the name of their band at the top of the schedule. Elicit a few questions and answers, trying to include examples of *at/in/on*, e.g. *What are they doing on Wednesday morning? They're travelling to New York. Are they arriving at JFK airport at three p.m. on Wednesday? Yes, they are. What are they doing in the evening? They're arriving at the hotel at six p.m.*
5 As students do the task, monitor and note any mistakes to correct at the end. When they have finished, ask them how many differences they found.

ANSWER KEY

There are eight differences:

Wednesday	A:	In the evening, they are meeting fans and signing autographs.
	B:	In the evening, they are relaxing in the hotel.
Thursday	A:	At 10 a.m., they are appearing on a TV show.
	B:	At 10 a.m., they are appearing on a radio show.
	A:	At 7 p.m., they're flying to Los Angeles.
	B:	At 7 p.m., they're flying to San Francisco.
Friday	A:	In the afternoon, they are giving an interview for radio.
	B:	In the afternoon, they are giving an interview for television.
	A:	At 10 p.m., they are opening a new bar.
	B:	At 10 p.m., they are opening a new club.
Saturday	A:	In the morning, they are going shopping.
	B:	In the morning, they are visiting the city.
	A:	At 8 p.m., they are having dinner in the hotel.
	B:	At 8 p.m., they are having a drink in the hotel.
Sunday	A:	In the afternoon, they are watching an American football match.
	B:	In the afternoon, they are playing football.

Sheet A

Schedule for publicity tour of USA – first version

	Wednesday	Thursday	Friday	Saturday	Sunday
Morning	Travel to New York	10 a.m. Appear on a TV show	Make a video	Go shopping	Relax in the hotel
Afternoon	3 p.m. Arrive at JFK airport Have a press conference	3 p.m. Open a record shop Give a magazine interview	2 p.m. Meet the President 4 p.m. Give an interview for radio	Play a concert in the park Meet fans and sign autographs	1 p.m. Have lunch Watch an American football match
Evening	6 p.m. Arrive at hotel Meet fans and sign autographs	7 p.m. Fly to Los Angeles 10 p.m. Arrive at the hotel	Eat in a famous restaurant 10 p.m. Open a new bar	8 p.m. Eat dinner in the hotel 11 p.m. Perform at a club	7 p.m. Have a press conference Come home

Sheet B

Schedule for publicity tour of USA – revised version

	Wednesday	Thursday	Friday	Saturday	Sunday
Morning	Travel to New York	10 a.m. Appear on a radio show	Make a video	Visit the city	Relax in the hotel
Afternoon	3 p.m. Arrive at JFK airport Have a press conference	3 p.m. Open a record shop Give a magazine interview	2 p.m. Meet the President 4 p.m. Give an interview for television	Play a concert in the park Meet fans and sign autographs	1 p.m. Have lunch Play football
Evening	6 p.m. Arrive at hotel Relax in the hotel	7 p.m. Fly to San Francisco 10 p.m. Arrive at hotel	Eat dinner in a famous restaurant 10 p.m. Open a new club	8 p.m. Have a drink in the hotel 11 p.m. Perform at a club	7 p.m. Have a press conference Come home

Vocabulary Adjectives and their opposites
Grammar *So* + adjective / *such* + noun
Language to go Emphasising feelings and opinions

It's such a good game!

Aim

To practise *so* + adjective, *such* + noun and adjectives of opinion

Materials

One copy of the sheet, one coin and four counters per group of four

Time

30 minutes

Preparation

Copy the sheet as above

Procedure

1 Divide students into groups of four (or three, if necessary). Hand out a copy of the game board, a coin and four counters to each group.
2 Ask the students to put their counters on the Start / Finish square. Explain the rules:
   • The aim is to move around the board by tossing the coin. Heads = move forward one square, tails = move forward two squares.
   • When a student lands on a square, he / she should toss the coin again; this time, heads = *so*, tails = *such*. The student then makes a sentence about the subject on the square with *so* or *such*, e.g. for Square 1: *The meal in the restaurant was so delicious / it was such a delicious meal.*
   • If the answer is grammatically correct according to the other students, the student goes forward one square. If it is incorrect, he / she stays on the square. Play then passes to the next student.
   • The winner is the first student to reach the finish.
3 Before they start, elicit a couple of examples from a strong group. While students play the game, monitor and settle any disputes.

Alternative

With a strong class, the student to the right of the student who made the sentence can ask a follow-up question, for example:
Student 1: *The meal in the restaurant was so delicious.*
Student 2: *Really? What did you eat?*
Student 1: *I ate a lovely steak with salad.*
If you are going to attempt this, make sure it is demonstrated at the start so that students are clear about what they are doing.

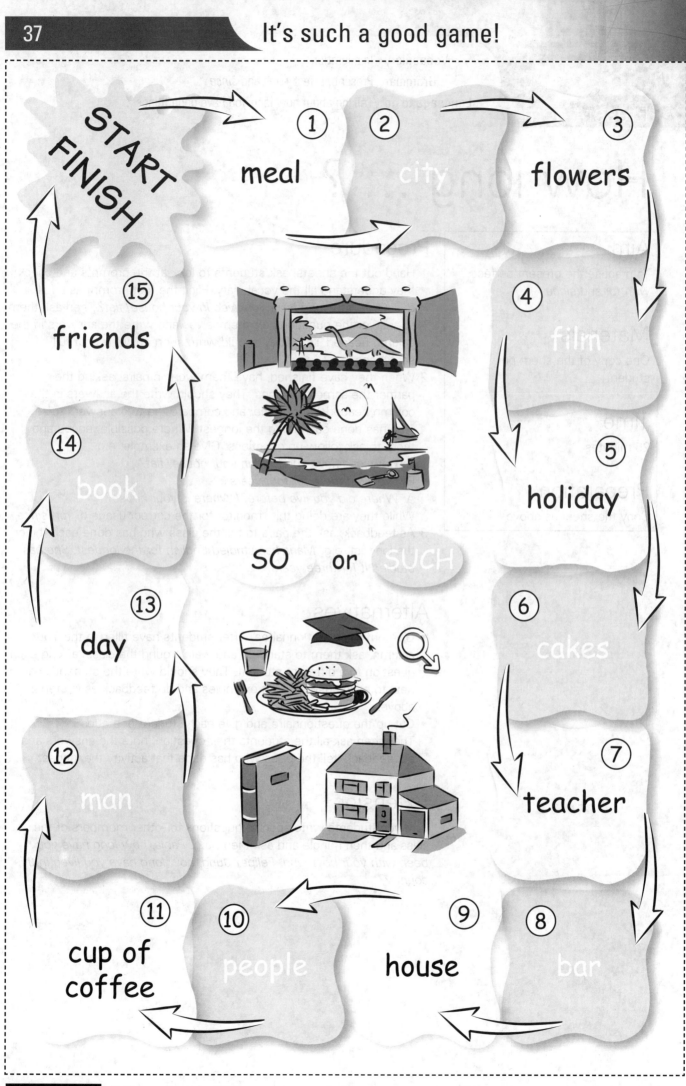

START
FINISH

① meal

② city

③ flowers

④ film

⑤ holiday

⑥ cakes

⑦ teacher

⑧ bar

⑨ house

⑩ people

⑪ cup of coffee

⑫ man

⑬ day

⑭ book

⑮ friends

SO   or   SUCH

Vocabulary   Immigration
Grammar   Present perfect + *for* and *since*
Language to go   Talking about how long you have done things

How long ... ?

Aim

To practise the present perfect with *for* and *since*

Materials

One copy of the sheet per student

Time

25 minutes

Preparation

Copy the sheet as above

Procedure

1 Hand out the sheets, ask students to look at the prompts and check they understand all the vocabulary. Elicit the first prompt as a full question: *How long have you lived in your house/ flat?* Then ask them to answer the questions for themselves and write the answers in the column headed *You*. They should write short answers, not full sentences.

2 When they have finished, have them work in pairs, asking their partner the same questions. They should write the answers in the column headed *Your partner* and compare the two answers to see who has done each thing the longest. Where possible, encourage them to ask follow-up questions. Give an example, e.g.
   A: *How long have you lived in your house/ flat?*
   B: *I've lived there for four years.*
   A: *Where did you live before?/ Where is your house?*
   While they are doing this, monitor for the correct usage of *for/ since*.

3 As feedback, ask the pairs to tell the class who has done each thing the longest, e.g. *Maria has studied English for the longest. She has studied it for three years.*

Alternatives

• Give out the questionnaires. After students have filled in the *You* column, ask them to stand up and walk around the class, asking each question to a different student. They should write the student's name next to each answer. Elicit examples and do feedback as in step 2 above.

• Cut up the questionnaire and give each student one question.
  They then ask all the students their question, note the answers and as feedback, tell the class who has done that activity the longest.

Extension

Writing: Students write specific questions for other members of the class and then mingle and ask them, e.g. *Paola, how long have you been with your boyfriend, Felipe? Jung, how long have you lived in this country?*

How long … ?

How long … ?	You	Your partner
(live) in your house / flat?		
(study) English?		
(be) in this class?		
(have) the same hairstyle?		
(know) your best friend?		
(have) your driving licence?		
(know) how to read?		
(work) in your present company / (study) at your present school?		
(like) your favourite musician?		
(be) awake today?		

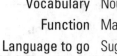

Vocabulary Nouns and verbs: word building
Function Making and responding to suggestions
Language to go Suggesting solutions to problems

Problems, problems

Aim

To practise making suggestions using *Why don't we … ? Shall we … ? Let's … How/What about + -ing*

Materials

One copy of the sheet per group of four

Time

25 minutes

Preparation

Copy the sheet as above (onto card if possible) and cut up into ten squares

Procedure

1 Ask students to think of times they have had to make decisions/solve problems with other people. *Who are the other people e.g. friends, colleagues, family, classmates … ?*
2 Put students into groups of four and hand out one set of cards per group. Explain that they have to take it in turns to turn over one of their cards and read out the situation/problem. Then each student has to make a suggestion to solve the problem (including the student who read out the situation); they should discuss the solutions and agree on the best one. Suggestions for the first card could be *Why don't we buy her a present? Let's have a party. Shall we go to the pub? How about buying her some flowers?*
3 While students discuss their problems, monitor and help with vocabulary, correcting where necessary.
4 As feedback, read out some of the situations and ask what each group decided.

You are classmates. You have a great teacher, and it's her birthday tomorrow. You would like to buy her something special.

You are all colleagues. You feel that you work very hard and you are not getting paid enough.

You're all studying English, and there is an important test in the next lesson.

You want to have a house party for the birthday of one of your friends, but are worried that the neighbours will complain if you make a lot of noise.

You all live together in the same flat. Your neighbour plays music very loudly early in the morning and wakes everybody up.

You are a family who would like to go on a day trip. You need to do something that makes everybody happy.

You all work together in the same company. One of your colleagues is very lazy and never does any work. This means that you all have to work harder.

You are a group of friends. One of your other friends is feeling very depressed and you would like to help.

You are a group of friends who would like to go on holiday together. The only problem is that you haven't got very much money.

You're all doing an English course together and tomorrow is the last lesson.

Vocabulary	Parties
Grammar	Second conditional (*if* + past simple + *would*/*could*)
Language to go	Talking about imaginary situations

What would you do?

Aim

To practise the second conditional for talking about imaginary situations

Materials

One copy of the sheet per class (two copies if more than fourteen students in the class)

Time

25–30 minutes

Preparation

Copy the sheet as above and cut it into fourteen cards

Procedure

1 Write on the board *What/ do/ if/ win a million pounds* and elicit the full question (*What would you do if you won a million pounds?*). Now ask a few students round the class this question. Try to encourage *I'd* … rather than a repetition of the whole question, i.e. *If I won a million pounds, I'd* …

2 If you have more than fourteen students, either duplicate some of the cards or divide the students into two groups, with a set of cards for each group.

3 Give each student one of the prompt cards.

4 Ask students to look at their prompt card and make sure they know how to form the question. Monitor and answer any questions about vocabulary/forming the question.

5 Without looking at their prompt card, students should walk around the classroom asking each other the questions.

6 After ten minutes (or when the students have asked everyone in the class), they should sit back down and try and remember what some of the answers were. Use the example at the beginning to illustrate this, e.g. *If Maria won a million pounds, she'd buy a new house. Yumiko would travel the world. Simone would start her own business* (don't keep repeating the *if* clause – this would be too boring). Students should try and write as many as they can remember. Monitor and correct if necessary.

7 Put the students in pairs so that they can tell their partner their sentences.

8 As feedback, ask how many sentences each person managed to write and ask each student to tell the class their most interesting answer.

Extension

Writing: In pairs, students write three questions of their own to ask another pair.

What would you do?

What / do / if / speak fluent English?

If / go to a fancy dress party / what / wear?

Where / live / if / can live / anywhere in the world?

What type of music / play / if / be in a band?

What / do / if / not have to work?

If / have a yacht / where / go?

If / can learn any other language / which / choose?

If money / be no problem / where / go on holiday?

What / say / if / meet the Queen?

What / do / if / have more free time?

Which famous person / invite / if / have a dinner party?

If / be / your birthday today / what / do?

If / see a UFO / what / do?

If / can choose the perfect job / what / it be?

Test 1

Grammar

1 Complete the advert. Expand the notes to make sentences.

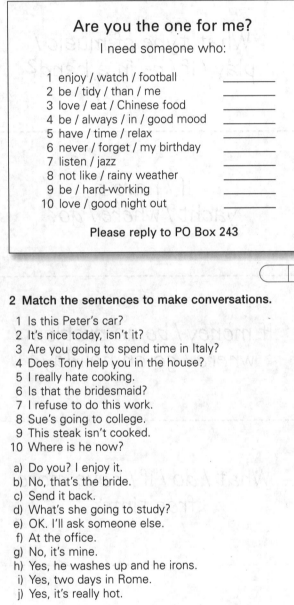

Are you the one for me?

I need someone who:

1 enjoy / watch / football   _____
2 be / tidy / than / me   _____
3 love / eat / Chinese food   _____
4 be / always / in / good mood   _____
5 have / time / relax   _____
6 never / forget / my birthday   _____
7 listen / jazz   _____
8 not like / rainy weather   _____
9 be / hard-working   _____
10 love / good night out   _____

Please reply to PO Box 243

| 10 |

2 Match the sentences to make conversations.

1 Is this Peter's car?
2 It's nice today, isn't it?
3 Are you going to spend time in Italy?
4 Does Tony help you in the house?
5 I really hate cooking.
6 Is that the bridesmaid?
7 I refuse to do this work.
8 Sue's going to college.
9 This steak isn't cooked.
10 Where is he now?

a) Do you? I enjoy it.
b) No, that's the bride.
c) Send it back.
d) What's she going to study?
e) OK. I'll ask someone else.
f) At the office.
g) No, it's mine.
h) Yes, he washes up and he irons.
i) Yes, two days in Rome.
j) Yes, it's really hot.

1 _____   2 _____   3 _____   4 _____   5 _____
6 _____   7 _____   8 _____   9 _____   10 _____

| 10 |

3 Complete the second sentences so that they mean the same as the first sentences. Use the correct form of the words in brackets.

1 Do not park here. It's against the law.
   You _____ . (must)
2 This child is very talkative.
   This child _____ . (a lot)
3 Sam isn't as aggressive as his brother.
   Sam _____ . (less)
4 Tennis balls can be bought from the hotel reception.
   You can _____ . (buy)
5 If you are over eighteen, you can join the social club.
   Unless you are over eighteen, _____ . (can)

| 5 |

4 Choose the best options to complete the text.

When I was a teenager, just before I (1) _____ to university, I decided to go travelling. I went to Israel with a friend to work on a melon farm. It was great fun, although the work was quite hard. We (2) _____ at five every morning and go by truck to the melon fields to pick melons. We had to start very early because the south of Israel is (3) _____ hot, so hot in fact that we used to feel exhausted by the end of the morning. We had every afternoon free, which gave us plenty of (4) _____ to relax. My friend liked (5) _____ the area, so we often went up into the mountains, or into the desert. We also learnt to scuba (6) _____ . The first time we looked underwater, we were amazed. I (7) _____ anything so beautiful since then.

In those days, it wasn't possible to (8) _____ an e-mail to our parents back at home. They were always worried. They thought we (9) _____ too many risks. We wrote lots of postcards and (10) _____ phone calls once a month to reassure them.

 1 a) go   b) went
    c) am going   d) have gone
 2 a) have got up   b) get up
    c) are getting up   d) used to get up
 3 a) absolutely   b) mostly
    c) particularly   d) totally
 4 a) amounts   b) possibility
    c) chance   d) time
 5 a) explore   b) exploratory
    c) exploring   d) exploration
 6 a) dive   b) swim
    c) fish   d) jump
 7 a) am not seeing   b) don't see
    c) won't see   d) haven't seen
 8 a) make   b) send
    c) post   d) take
 9 a) are taking   b) have taken
    c) take   d) took
10 a) made   b) did
    c) sent   d) answered

| 10 |

5 Tick (✓) the correct sentences.

1 a) Did you enjoy your holiday last month? ☐
   b) Have you enjoyed your holiday last month? ☐
2 a) Peter enjoys to dance. ☐
   b) Peter enjoys dancing. ☐
3 a) The groom shouldn't to see the bride before
      the wedding. ☐
   b) The groom shouldn't see the bride before
      the wedding. ☐
4 a) I'm usually going to the beach on Wednesdays. ☐
   b) I usually go to the beach on Wednesdays. ☐
5 a) Come and sit down. We watch a video. ☐
   b) Come and sit down. We're watching a video. ☐
6 a) If you go out, please take the dog. ☐
   b) If you will go out, please take the dog. ☐
7 a) That mini-disc belongs to Pat. ☐
   b) That mini-disc is belonging to Pat. ☐
8 a) Look! It rains. ☐
   b) Look! It's raining. ☐
9 a) If you don't like the shirt, you can send it back. ☐
   b) If you won't like the shirt, you can send it back. ☐
10 a) Did you see Johnny yesterday? ☐
    b) Have you seen Johnny yesterday? ☐

⬭ 10

Vocabulary

6 Ten of the words in this text are incorrect. Find them and replace them with the words in the box.

honeymoon ring ceremony list wedding
reception newly traditional best bride's

Vanessa and David are very excited. (1) Next
Saturday is their ceremony day. (2) David
has chosen Paul to be his great man. (3) It's
Paul's job to look after the cake, (4) so that
David can put it on his groom's finger.
(5) As usual, many of the guests want to
give presents to the freshly-married
couple. (6) Because of this, Vanessa and
David have a wedding sheet for their
friends to choose from. (7) They are going
to have a festival wedding in a church,
(8) and when the tradition is finished,
(9) there's going to be a big ring in a hotel.
(10) And when it's all over, they're going to
leave for their journey.

⬭ 10

7 Underline the correct options.

1 I often *say* / *send* / *post* faxes.
2 My colleague loves *making* / *organising* / *taking*
   conferences.
3 Can you *arrange* / *deliver* / *take* a meeting at ten o'clock?
4 You should *ask* / *say* / *tell* sorry. You're very late.
5 My boss *made* / *got* / *felt* married last Saturday.
6 You *have* / *ought* / *should* send it by e-mail. It's quicker.
7 He's going to *book* / *ask* / *call* the flight tickets.
8 Do you like *dividing* / *sharing* / *cutting* your job?
9 Don't worry. I'll *examine* / *test* / *check* the train times.
10 I wish my children *behaved* / *became* / *took* better.

⬭ 10

8 Choose a category (A–E) for each sentence (1–15).

A At the office
B The weather
C Holidays
D Sports
E People's personalities

1 I think I'll try a bit of water skiing this weekend.
2 The hurricane destroyed a lot of the buildings.
3 Please behave yourself this time.
4 How about going on a cruise next year?
5 What time do you usually leave work?
6 Did you know Chris ran a half-marathon yesterday?
7 It was wonderful. We stayed in luxury accommodation.
8 You can use the laptop if you like.
9 He can be quite aggressive.
10 It is going to be cloudy with a bit of sun in the afternoon.
11 Shall we do some rock-climbing?
12 Could you photocopy this for me?
13 Many people are competitive.
14 The average temperature in June is 25 degrees.
15 We went on a safari and saw lions and tigers.

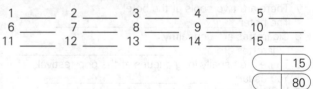

1 ____	2 ____	3 ____	4 ____	5 ____
6 ____	7 ____	8 ____	9 ____	10 ____
11 ____	12 ____	13 ____	14 ____	15 ____

⬭ 15

⬭ 80

Test 2

Grammar

1 Correct the mistakes in both parts of the dialogues.

1 Fred: Don't you make that cake yet?
  Natalie: No, I didn't. I need some sugar.
2 Scott: There isn't some coffee left.
  Frances: Isn't there? OK, I'm going to buy some.
3 Alan: Why aren't you sleeping well last night?
  Mandy: I don't know. I just couldn't sleep in spite I was tired.
4 Richard: I am going down the street when I saw a robbery.
  Mark: Really? What have you done? Did you call the police?
5 Nina: Look! This computer made in China.
  John: That's strange. I thought it is made in Japan.

                                  (10)

2 Complete the second sentences so that they mean the same as the first sentences.

1 Sarah had long hair, but she doesn't have long hair now.
  She _____ .
2 Peter doesn't live with anyone.
  He lives on _____ .
3 You needn't wear formal clothes to the meeting.
  You don't _____ .
4 This clothes shop is trendier than any other in the town.
  It's the _____ .
5 James couldn't speak French at all when he joined.
  James was no _____ .
6 When I was young, I hated coffee. Now I love it.
  I didn't _____ .
7 There are two pools at the hotel.
  The hotel _____ .
8 Cigarettes are unhealthy.
  Cigarettes are bad _____ .
9 There are usually long queues at the pop festival.
  You usually _____ .
10 If Charlie won't look after the dog, I won't go.
  Unless Charlie _____ .

                                  (10)

3 Underline the correct options.

I remember when we lived in Waterloo, a small town outside Brussels, we (1) *used to go / have gone* to the tiny sweet shop after school every day (2) *for / buy* some sweets. We (3) *have / had* to wear school uniform in those days, and we both (4) *carry / used to carry* our schoolbags on our backs. Neither my brother nor I (5) *could / can* really speak much French, but the shopkeeper was always kind to us.

Our teachers didn't speak (6) *any / some* English, but both of us were good (7) *in / at* languages, so we quickly (8) *learnt / used to learn* to speak to our friends in French.

I'm going back to Waterloo next month, twenty years after I left the school. I hope it (9) *is looking / will look* just the same as it did then. I hope there (10) *has been / will be* a sweet shop and a little old lady waiting to take my money and give me a lollipop.

                                  (10)

4 Choose the best options to complete the e-mail.

Hi, Alan

Did you see last night's (1) _____ of *Beat Street*? What a fantastic story! Sarah thinks her heart (2) _____ because Jason has left her and Guy says he (3) _____ her again if she speaks to Jason. I think Jason will come back and then Sarah (4) _____ to marry him. Anyway, I (5) _____ it on video if you want it.

Do you remember I (6) _____ make my Internet connection work properly? It's OK now. I used to have it connected to my parents' phone line, but now I've got my own line in my bedroom. Cool, huh? I (7) _____ for the day when I can live on my own. Parents (8) _____ you crazy. I even (9) _____ babysit Julie last night! Terrible. I gave her loads of sweets (10) _____ I wanted to watch TV in peace.

Jim

1 a) programme   b) episode
  c) series   d) chapter
2 a) breaks   b) break
  c) will break   d) breaking
3 a) doesn't   b) didn't see
  c) hasn't seen   d) won't see
4 a) is promising   b) will promise
  c) promise   d) promised
5 a) have got   b) am having
  c) have had   d) had
6 a) can't   b) won't be able to
  c) couldn't   d) haven't
7 a) don't wait   b) won't wait
  c) haven't waited   d) can't wait
8 a) are driving   b) drive
  c) drove   d) have driven
9 a) must   b) have to
  c) must to   d) had to
10 a) because   b) in order
  c) although   d) despite

                                  (10)

5 Match the two parts of the sentences and connect them using one of the words in the box.

at	will	or	for	already	to	if	of	for	any

1 Has he
2 Louise went to the chemist's
3 Hannah doesn't think she
4 We didn't use
5 Have you got
6 I was very good
7 I'll join the gym
8 Club membership is free
9 Chocolate is bad
10 Are you married

a) phoned Michelle?
b) milk I can borrow?
c) some aspirins.
d) you.
e) marry Andrew.
f) single?
g) go to the cinema.
h) you come with me.
i) maths when I was younger.
j) charge.

1 _____   2 _____   3 _____   4 _____   5 _____
6 _____   7 _____   8 _____   9 _____   10 _____

                                  (20)

6 Read the text and say whether the sentences are *True* or *False*.

When I was young, I wasn't very good at sports. I used to try to escape when it was time to play tennis or hockey. My teachers often caught me and sent me back to play. Nowadays, I'm the opposite. I'm a professional tennis player, and although I haven't won Wimbledon yet, I believe I will one day. I have already contacted some advertising companies. You can get a lot of things for free that way. I used to think that all sports personalities had easy lives. Now I know that's not true. I have to work extremely hard, but I must say I love it.

	True	False
1 The speaker was not good at tennis as a child.	☐	☐
2 The speaker often escaped from home.	☐	☐
3 He liked hockey but hated tennis.	☐	☐
4 His teachers made him do sports.	☐	☐
5 The speaker is hoping to become a professional player.	☐	☐
6 He has not won Wimbledon.	☐	☐
7 He hasn't yet contacted any advertising companies.	☐	☐
8 He works for free.	☐	☐
9 Sports personalities have difficult lives.	☐	☐
10 He hates his job.	☐	☐

⬭ 10

Vocabulary

7 Put sentences A–E in this letter into the correct order, then do the same with sentences F–J.

Dear Sir

A Last month I used your travel agency to
B you sent me to the wrong terminal, so I
C arrived late for the flight.
D for the airport at nine o'clock as you suggested. Unfortunately,
E book a holiday in Jamaica. I left

F Your advertising says that you are the most
G to let me rent one. And the resort is not
H efficient travel agency in the town. However, when I tried to rent
I the trendiest one on the island, as you said.
J a car, the company said that you were terrible and refused

I would be grateful if you would arrange to call me soon to discuss this.

Yours faithfully

J.M. Davies

---

1 _____ 2 _____ 3 _____ 4 _____ 5 _____
6 _____ 7 _____ 8 _____ 9 _____ 10 _____

⬭ 10

8 Underline the correct options.

1 Do you ever wear *tall* / *high* heels?
2 Frank lives *on* / *by* his own.
3 Jack is our *same* / *mutual* friend.
4 Have you met Sid? He's a *heavy* / *heavyweight* champion.
5 What you said gave me *ideas* / *food* for thought.
6 Is there a *convenience* / *usefulness* store near here?
7 Did he *transform* / *convert* to Islam?
8 I've just *received* / *caught* your e-mail.
9 I love watching *soaps* / *soups* on TV.
10 Eating too much sugar *does* / *'makes* you fat.

⬭ 10

9 Tick (✓) the correct options.

1 If your car is *reliable*, does it work well?
   a) Yes. ☐
   b) No. ☐
2 Can you use *much* with countable nouns?
   a) Yes. ☐
   b) No. ☐
3 Which sentence is correct?
   a) Did you find my book yesterday? ☐
   b) Have you found my book yesterday? ☐
4 A sauna is a:
   a) hot place. ☐
   b) cold place. ☐
5 If you *used to* eat a lot of chocolate, do you still eat a lot of it?
   a) Yes. ☐
   b) No. ☐
6 Are sneakers:
   a) office shoes? ☐
   b) sports / informal shoes? ☐
7 If you *don't have to* get up early, is it necessary to get up early?
   a) Yes. ☐
   b) No. ☐
8 If you're *no good* at something, do you do it:
   a) well? ☐
   b) badly? ☐
9 Which sentence is correct?
   a) I've got a shower every day. ☐
   b) I have a shower every day. ☐
10 If you *dress down*, do you wear a tie?
   a) Yes. ☐
   b) No. ☐

⬭ 10
⬭ 100

Test 3

Grammar

1 Expand the notes to make new sentences using the correct tense.

1 We / rearrange / the office / yesterday.
_____

2 John / just / move / the desk. Now / it / nearer / the window.
_____

3 Tomorrow / we / buy / some plants.
_____

4 We / not hang / the / new / pictures / yet.
_____

5 Mary / already / do / all the filing.
_____

6 If / we / replace / the lights / next week, / the office / look / brighter.
_____

7 We / like / to buy / a new computer / but / they / be / expensive.
_____

8 Look! / John / just / clean / windows.
_____

9 We / be / tidy up / when / the boss / arrive.
_____

10 I / think / he / be / pleased / when / we / finish / tomorrow.
_____

⌐ 10 ⌐

2 Tick (✓) the correct sentences.

1 a) I'm so boring – there's nothing to do! ☐
  b) I'm so bored – there's nothing to do! ☐
2 a) I was amazed when I saw Pete. He looked so old. ☐
  b) I was amazing when I saw Pete. He looked so old. ☐
3 a) 'I've got terrible toothache.'
    'Have you? I'm going to get you an aspirin.' ☐
  b) 'I've got terrible toothache.'
    'Have you? I'll get you an aspirin.' ☐
4 a) I would marry you tomorrow if you asked me to. ☐
  b) I will marry you tomorrow if you asked me to. ☐
5 a) It's shocking how many homeless people there are. ☐
  b) It's shocked how many homeless people there are. ☐
6 a) Do you have to wear a uniform for your job? ☐
  b) Do you must wear a uniform for your job? ☐
7 a) I have given up smoking last week and I feel great. ☐
  b) I gave up smoking last week and I feel great. ☐
8 a) I'd like to be a waiter – you meet all sorts of interesting people. ☐
  b) I like be a waiter – you meet all sorts of interesting people. ☐
9 a) Hey! You don't have to park there. It's not allowed. ☐
  b) Hey! You can't park there. It's not allowed. ☐
10 a) I was asking a question when she interrupted me. ☐
  b) I am asking a question when she interrupted me. ☐

⌐ 10 ⌐

3 Complete the second sentences so that they mean the same as the first sentences. Use the words in brackets.

1 They make these jackets in Turkey.
  These jackets _____ . (made)
2 It isn't necessary for you to do the washing-up.
  You don't _____ . (have)
3 I've decided to go to Mexico on holiday.
  I _____ . (planning)
4 I can't play the drums. It would be nice to learn.
  I'd _____ . (like)
5 The car is clean.
  Peter has · _____ . (wash)
6 Your headaches worry me.
  Your headaches _____ . (worrying)
7 Don't carry heavy boxes. It's dangerous.
  You _____ . (mustn't)
8 Cooking is great fun.
  I really _____ . (enjoy)
9 Is it necessary for you to shout so loudly?
  Do you _____ . (have)
10 I don't know where they make these computers.
  Where are _____ ? (made)

⌐ 10 ⌐

4 Put the sentences in this e-mail in the correct order.

> **Myles! Where have you been? Why don't you e-mail me?**
>
> A **I've got news for you. I'm going to become**
> B **TV the other day when I saw a really**
> C **food. Then I'll invite you to dinner!**
> D **of all kinds of horrible ingredients? I've given**
> E **going to go shopping for some nice vegetarian**
> F **shocking programme about meat**
> G **a vegetarian. I was watching**
> H **up eating chicken already, and tomorrow I'm**
> I **products. Did you know most burgers are made**
>
> **Chaz**

1 _____ 2 _____ 3 _____ 4 _____ 5 _____
6 _____ 7 _____ 8 _____ 9 _____

⌐ 9 ⌐

140

5 Match the sentences to make conversations.

1 The phone's ringing.
2 I've just washed the car.
3 Is it OK if I call Paul?
4 What would you do?
5 You mustn't eat those mushrooms.
6 I'm going to go for a swim.
7 Have you already written your e-mail?
8 Can I smoke here?
9 I went to New Jersey yesterday.
10 I have to be home by midnight.

a) OK, have a nice time.
b) Why? Are they poisonous?
c) No, I'm afraid it isn't allowed.
d) Yes, I've just sent it.
e) Did you have a good journey?
f) That's fine. I'll give you a lift.
g) Don't worry, I'll answer it.
h) Yes, of course it is.
i) I think I'd apologise.
j) Thanks. It looks very clean.

1 _____ 2 _____ 3 _____ 4 _____ 5 _____
6 _____ 7 _____ 8 _____ 9 _____ 10 _____

10

Vocabulary

6 Underline the correct options.

1 A: So, what's your idea of the *perfect* / *good* job?
   B: One which gives me *activity* / *responsibility*.
2 A: Do you want a *career* / *task* in sales?
   B: Yes, I do. And I want to earn a good *payment* / *salary*.
3 A: Would you like to work *for* / *with* animals?
   B: No. I *rather* / *would like* to work in a big office.
4 A: What's wrong? You look *sick* / *sickening*.
   B: I've got a very *aching* / *sore* throat.
5 A: Do you enjoy working *lonely* / *alone*?
   B: Yes, it's quite *interested* / *interesting* in a way.
6 A: Have you *turned* / *changed* your mind about getting married?
   B: No, not at all. I just want you to tell the *honesty* / *truth*.
7 A: This play is the *longest-running* / *longest-walking* play on Broadway.
   B: Is it? I'm not *surprising* / *surprised*. It's very good.
8 A: Have you got a cold? You're *puffing* / *blowing* your nose a lot.
   B: No, I've got an *allergic* / *allergy* to flowers. They make me sneeze.
9 A: I hear that Chicago is full of street *gangs* / *teams*.
   B: No, it's not! Who *said* / *told* you that?
10 A: It's our wedding *birthday* / *anniversary* today.
   B: I know it is. I've bought you a *real* / *true* gold bracelet.

20

7 Eleven of the words in this text are incorrect. Replace them with the words in the box.

stomachache	creative	composer	house
leather	no-smoking	researcher	musical
cinema	station	mechanic	

(1) Richard is a car mend. He has a girlfriend called Polly.
(2) They live close to the police farm, in the centre of Birmingham. (3) Polly works for a publishing company as a picture finder. Her job is to find photographs to illustrate books. (4) You need to be quite creating to do the job well.
(5) Richard and Polly have just moved habitation and plan to get married next year.

(6) As a surprise, Richard booked two tickets for a cartoon called *Phantom of the Opera* last week. Polly always enjoys them. (7) The inventor of this one is Andrew Lloyd Webber. Unfortunately, the evening didn't go very well.
(8) First, there was no room in the cigaretteless area of the theatre bar. (9) Then, in the middle of the evening, Polly got a very bad stomachrash, (10) and Richard tore his plastic jacket on the car door. It didn't matter, though.
(11) They both laughed about it afterwards and decided to go to the filmhouse next time.

11

8 Tick (✓) the correct options.

1 Do you make a pre-nuptial agreement:
   a) before your wedding? ☐
   b) after your wedding? ☐
2 Do you:
   a) lose your temper? ☐
   b) waste your temper? ☐
3 Snapping your fingers in a restaurant in the UK is considered:
   a) polite. ☐
   b) rude. ☐
4 Do you:
   a) tell the truth? ☐
   b) say the truth? ☐
5 Which sentence is correct?
   a) I feel awful. I depressed. ☐
   b) I feel awful. I'm depressed. ☐
6 Do you:
   a) ask for permission? ☐
   b) seek for permission? ☐
7 Which sentence is correct?
   a) May I open the window? ☐
   b) I can open the window? ☐
8 If you eat meat, are you a *vegetarian*?
   a) Yes. ☐
   b) No. ☐
9 Is this sentence correct?
   I love be a teacher; it's the best job in the world.
   a) Yes. ☐
   b) No. ☐
10 If you work from home, do you have to wear a suit?
   a) Yes. ☐
   b) No. ☐

10

90

Test 4

Grammar

1 Underline the correct options.

1 A: How long *do you live* / *have you lived* in the USA?
   B: Since I *started* / *start* working at Disneyland.
2 A: *Do* / *Did* you find it difficult to get a work permit?
   B: No. I *will marry* / *am married* to an American.
3 A: How long *have you known* / *do you know* your wife?
   B: Oh, *for* / *since* ages! We *have met* / *met* in 1983.
4 A: If you could do any job in the world, what *will* / *would* it be?
   B: I think I *like* / *would like* to fly aeroplanes.
5 A: It *can* / *must* be fun to work at Disneyland.
   B: Yes, most of the time it *will be* / *is*.
6 A: *Are you planning* / *Do you plan* anything for the summer holidays?
   B: Yes. We *take* / *are taking* the children to the UK for the first time.
7 A: *Have* / *Did* they ever been out of the USA before?
   B: Only once. In 2000, we *were taking* / *took* them to Canada.
8 A: Do they want to *travel* / *travelling* more?
   B: Yes, I *think* / *I'm thinking* so.
9 A: If they *could* / *can* go anywhere, where would they choose?
   B: They *will* / *would* go to India. They are fascinated by it!
10 A: *Have you been* / *Were you* happier since you moved to the States?
   B: I *am* / *was* always happy wherever I am.

[20]

2 Correct the mistakes in these sentences.
Be careful – some of the sentences are correct!

1 If I have a lot of free time, I'd take up a new hobby.
2 I meet a friend for coffee later.
3 Most cars are imported.
4 A photocopier is a machine who copies things.
5 John isn't at home. He might be at the office.
6 Let's we go somewhere nice this weekend.
7 I've decided to cut down on fatty food.
8 The murderer is executed last week.
9 Who did help you with your work?
10 The concert was so good fun.

[10]

3 Underline the correct options.

1 My sister has decided *giving up* / *to give up* smoking.
2 Let's carry on *to work* / *working* until six.
3 That *must* / *can't* be James – he's not here this week.
4 Tom is *so* / *such* good-looking, I think I've fallen in love with him.
5 Shakespeare *has written* / *wrote* plays.
6 That *can't* / *must* be a spider. It's only got six legs, and spiders have eight.
7 That's the cash machine *that* / *where* I lost my bank card.
8 I haven't seen Valerie *since* / *for* years. I wonder how she is.
9 This is the house *where* / *which* I was born.
10 Why *haven't* / *didn't* you asked me to marry you yet?

[10]

4 Read the passage. Complete the sentences using the passive.

Did you hear what happened last night? Someone robbed the bank on the High Street. They stole over a million pounds. They forced open the door and they broke three windows. They opened the safe and took everything inside it. But that's not all. They stole two security vans. Then they drove them really fast down the motorway. The police chased the robbers. They didn't catch them.

1 The bank on the High Street _____ .
2 Over a million pounds _____ .
3 The door _____ .
4 Three windows _____ .
5 The safe _____ .
6 Everything inside it _____ .
7 Two security vans _____ .
8 The vans _____ .
9 The robbers _____ .
10 They _____ .

[10]

5 Write the dialogue using full sentences. Use *shall* in the questions and the words in brackets in the answers.

1 A: What / do?
   B: get married (let)
2 A: tell our friends?
   B: keep it a secret? (how)
3 A: send them a postcard?
   B: e-mail (let)
4 A: Where / go?
   B: somewhere romantic? (what)
5 A: somewhere hot or cold?
   B: visit / Greece (let)
6 A: stay in town or in country?
   B: a week in each (how)
7 A: How long for?
   B: away for a month (let)
8 A: by car or by plane?
   B: cycle? (what)
9 A: hotel or bed and breakfast?
   B: take / the tent? (how)
10 A: When / leave?
   B: straightaway! (let)

[10]

6 Complete the second sentences so that they mean the same as the first sentences. Use *can't*, *must* or *might*.

1 I'm certain he's Spanish.
   He _____ .
2 It's possible Petra's not well.
   Petra _____ .
3 I'm sure the garage isn't open today.
   The garage _____ .
4 It's possible Martin's on the train now.
   Martin _____ .
5 I'm sure the coffee's ready now.
   The coffee _____ .

[5]

Vocabulary

7 Complete the crossword.

Across

3 My new _____ TV is much better than my old analogue one.
7 When the Prime Minister arrived, he held a press _____ at the airport.
8 Jean must be really tired. She _____ all the time.
9 You use a _____ to type words into a computer.
10 The _____ is the machine you use to copy documents.

Down

1 To call his dog, he doesn't shout – he _____ .
2 Apparently there was a _____ here last week and they still haven't caught the mugger.
4 Have you seen my driving _____ anywhere?
5 Now that I've got a _____ , I can put my photos onto my computer.
6 You need a _____ permit before you can get a job in the USA.

[10]

8 Tick (✓) the correct options.

1 A burglar steals from people in the street.
   a) True. ☐
   b) False. ☐
2 Do you:
   a) spend a fine? ☐
   b) pay a fine? ☐
3 To emigrate to the USA, you need a:
   a) green card. ☐
   b) pink card. ☐
4 What would you do if someone gave you a *lager*?
   a) Eat it. ☐
   b) Wear it. ☐
   c) Drink it. ☐
5 People snore because they are tired.
   a) True. ☐
   b) False. ☐
6 Which sentence is correct?
   a) That's the mugger who was arrested. ☐
   b) That's the mugger which was arrested. ☐

7 Which sentence is correct?
   a) I've been here for three hours. ☐
   b) I've been here since three hours. ☐
8 A robber might steal from a bank.
   a) True. ☐
   b) False. ☐
9 A *laptop* is a:
   a) large computer. ☐
   b) small computer. ☐
10 You need *willpower* to go on a diet or to give up smoking.
   a) True. ☐
   b) False. ☐

[10]

9 Choose the correct options to complete this radio broadcast.

It's Saturday. No work to do and a huge choice of entertainment! Why not spend some (1) _____ with the family? Here are our recommendations for today.

At two o'clock at the football ground, the (2) _____ match between Leeds United and Arsenal kicks off. You'll hear the (3) _____ from the stadium as fans celebrate the winning goals. Further down the street, a (4) _____ band is playing a concert in the park at six p.m. When Robbie Watson steps on stage, the girls will (5) _____ and the boys will (6) _____ . Not a fan of pop? Don't worry. The youth centre is holding a (7) _____ party for the under-tens tonight, starting at seven. If you're hungry, you can enjoy a (8) _____ meal at the Green Man Restaurant, followed by a superb (9) _____ display, all for under fifteen pounds per person. There's a bonus for those of you who drive cars: (10) _____ drinks will be served free of charge all evening. Do more this weekend!

1	a) space	b) time
	c) energy	d) fun
2	a) large	b) enormous
	c) big	d) huge
3	a) cheering	b) whispering
	c) talking	d) waving
4	a) living	b) existing
	c) being	d) live
5	a) scream	b) read
	c) run	d) fight
6	a) jog	b) pull
	c) hit	d) clap
7	a) funny-dress	b) silly-dress
	c) fancy-dress	d) ridiculous-dress
8	a) three-piece	b) three-course
	c) three-part	d) three-plate
9	a) homework	b) housework
	c) firework	d) roadwork
10	a) alcohol-full	b) alcohol-free
	c) alcohol-less	d) alcohol-poor

[10]
[95]

Tests answer key

Test 1

1 1 enjoys watching football 2 is tidier than me
  3 loves eating Chinese food 4 is always in a good mood
  5 has time to relax 6 never forgets my birthday
  7 listens to jazz 8 doesn't like rainy weather
  9 is hard-working 10 loves a good night out

2 1 g 2 j 3 i 4 h 5 a 6 b 7 e 8 d 9 c 10 f

3 1 You mustn't park here.
  2 This child talks a lot.
  3 Sam is less aggressive than his brother.
  4 You can buy tennis balls from the hotel reception.
  5 Unless you are over eighteen, you can't join the social club.

4 1 b 2 d 3 c 4 d 5 c 6 a 7 d 8 b 9 d 10 a

5 1 a 2 b 3 b 4 b 5 b 6 a 7 a 8 b 9 a 10 a

6 1 Next Saturday is their ~~ceremony~~ *wedding* day.
  2 David has chosen Paul to be his ~~great~~ *best* man.
  3 It's Paul's job to look after the ~~cake~~ *ring*.
  4 so that David can put it on his ~~groom's~~ *bride's* finger.
  5 As usual, many of the guests want to give presents to the ~~freshly~~ *newly*-married couple.
  6 Because of this, Vanessa and David have a wedding ~~sheet~~ *list* for their friends to choose from.
  7 They are going to have a ~~festival~~ *traditional* wedding in a church,
  8 and when the ~~tradition~~ *ceremony* is finished,
  9 there's going to be a big ~~ring~~ *reception* in a hotel
  10 And when it's all over, they're going to leave for their ~~journey~~ *honeymoon*.

7 1 send 2 organising 3 arrange 4 say 5 got
  6 should 7 book 8 sharing 9 check 10 behaved

8 1 D 2 B 3 E 4 C 5 A 6 D 7 C 8 A 9 E
  10 B 11 D 12 A 13 E 14 B 15 C

Test 2

1 1 Fred: ~~Don't~~ *Haven't* you ~~make~~ *made* that cake yet?
    Natalie: No, I ~~didn't~~ *haven't*. I need some sugar.
  2 Scott: There isn't ~~some~~ *any* coffee left.
    Frances: Isn't there? OK, ~~I'm going to~~ *I'll* buy some.
  3 Alan: Why ~~aren't you sleeping~~ *didn't you sleep* well last night?
    Mandy: I don't know. I just couldn't sleep ~~in spite/ I was~~ *although I was/in spite of being* tired.
  4 Richard: I ~~am~~ *was* going down the street when I saw a robbery.
    Mark: Really? What ~~have you done~~ *did you do*? Did you call the police?
  5 Nina: Look! This computer *was* made in China.
    John: That's strange. I thought it ~~is~~ *was* made in Japan.

2 1 She used to have long hair.
  2 He lives on his own.
  3 You don't have to wear formal clothes to the meeting.
  4 It's the trendiest shop in the town.
  5 James was no good at French when he joined.
  6 I didn't use to like coffee.
  7 The hotel has (got) two pools.
  8 Cigarettes are bad for your health/for you.
  9 You usually have to queue for a long time at the pop festival.
  10 Unless Charlie looks after the dog, I won't go.

3 1 used to go 2 for 3 had 4 used to carry 5 could
  6 any 7 at 8 learnt 9 will look 10 will be

4 1 b 2 c 3 d 4 b 5 a 6 c 7 d 8 b 9 d 10 a

5 1 a Has he already phoned Michelle?
  2 c Louise went to the chemist's for some aspirins.
  3 e Hannah doesn't think she will marry Andrew.
  4 g We didn't use to go to the cinema.
  5 b Have you got any milk I can borrow?
  6 i I was very good at maths when I was younger.
  7 h I'll join the gym if you come with me.
  8 j Club membership is free of charge.
  9 d Chocolate is bad for you.
  10 f Are you married or single?

6 1 True 2 False 3 False 4 True 5 False 6 True
  7 False 8 False 9 True 10 False

7 1 A 2 E 3 D 4 B 5 C 6 F 7 H 8 J 9 G 10 I

8 1 high 2 on 3 mutual 4 heavyweight 5 food
  6 convenience 7 convert 8 received 9 soaps
  10 makes

9 1 a 2 b 3 a 4 a 5 b 6 b 7 b 8 b 9 b 10 b

Test 3

1 1 We rearranged the office yesterday.
2 John has just moved the desk. Now it's nearer the window.
3 Tomorrow we're going to buy some plants.
4 We haven't hung the new pictures yet.
5 Mary has already done all the filing.
6 If we replace the lights next week, the office will look brighter.
7 We'd like to buy a new computer but they're expensive.
8 Look! John has just cleaned the windows.
9 We were tidying up when the boss arrived.
10 I think he'll be pleased when we finish tomorrow.

2 1 b 2 a 3 b 4 a 5 a 6 a 7 b 8 a 9 b 10 a

3 1 These jackets are made in Turkey.
2 You don't have to do the washing-up.
3 I'm planning to go to Mexico on holiday.
4 I'd like to learn to play the drums.
5 Peter has washed the car.
6 Your headaches are worrying.
7 You mustn't carry heavy boxes.
8 I really enjoy cooking.
9 Do you have to shout so loudly?
10 Where are these computers made?

4 1 A 2 G 3 B 4 F 5 I 6 D 7 H 8 E 9 C

5 1 g 2 j 3 h 4 i 5 b 6 a 7 d 8 c 9 e 10 f

6 1 perfect; responsibility 2 career; salary 3 with; would like 4 sick; sore 5 alone; interesting
6 changed; truth 7 longest-running; surprised
8 blowing; allergy 9 gangs; told 10 anniversary; real

7 1 Richard is a car ~~mend~~ *mechanic*.
2 They live close to the police ~~farm~~ *station*, in the centre of Birmingham.
3 Polly works for a publishing company as a picture ~~finder~~ *researcher*.
4 You need to be quite ~~creating~~ *creative* to do the job well.
5 Richard and Polly have just moved ~~habitation~~ *house* and plan to get married next year.
6 As a surprise, Richard booked two tickets for a ~~cartoon~~ *musical* called *Phantom of the Opera* last week.
7 The ~~inventor~~ *composer* of this one is Andrew Lloyd Webber.
8 First, there was no room in the ~~cigaretteless~~ *no-smoking* area of the theatre bar.
9 Then, in the middle of the evening, Polly got a very bad ~~stomachrash~~ *stomachache*,
10 and Richard tore his ~~plastic~~ *leather* jacket on the car door.
11 They both laughed about it afterwards and decided to go to the ~~filmhouse~~ *cinema* next time.

8 1 a 2 a 3 b 4 a 5 b 6 a 7 a 8 b 9 b 10 b

Test 4

1 1 have you lived; started 2 Did; am married
3 have you known; for; met 4 would; would like
5 must; is 6 Are you planning; are taking
7 Have; took 8 travel; I think 9 could; would
10 Have you been; am

2 1 If I ~~have had~~ a lot of free time, I'd take up a new hobby.
2 ~~I meet~~ *I'm meeting* a friend for coffee later.
3 *correct*
4 A photocopier is a machine ~~who that~~ / *which* copies things.
5 *correct*
6 Let's ~~we~~ go somewhere nice this weekend.
7 *correct*
8 The murderer ~~is was~~ executed last week.
9 Who ~~did help~~ *helped* you with your work?
10 The concert was ~~so such~~ good fun.

3 1 to give up 2 working 3 can't 4 so 5 wrote
6 can't 7 where 8 for 9 where 10 haven't

4 1 The bank on the High Street was robbed.
2 Over a million pounds were / was stolen.
3 The door was forced open.
4 Three windows were broken.
5 The safe was opened.
6 Everything inside it was taken.
7 Two security vans were stolen.
8 The vans were driven really fast down the motorway.
9 The robbers were chased (by the police).
10 They weren't caught.

5 1 A: What shall we do?
   B: Let's get married.
2 A: Shall we tell our friends?
   B: No, how about keeping it a secret?
3 A: Shall we send them a postcard?
   B: No, let's e-mail them / send them an e-mail.
4 A: Where shall we go?
   B: What about somewhere romantic?
5 A: Shall we go somewhere hot or cold?
   B: Let's visit Greece.
6 A: Shall we stay in the town or in the country?
   B: How about spending a week in each?
7 A: How long shall we go for?
   B: Let's go away for a month.
8 A: Shall we go / travel by car or by plane?
   B: What about cycling?
9 A: Shall we stay in a hotel or a bed and breakfast?
   B: How about taking the tent?
10 A: When shall we leave?
   B: Let's go straightaway!

6 1 He must be Spanish.
2 Petra might not be well.
3 The garage can't be open today.
4 Martin might be on the train now.
5 The coffee must be ready now.

7 **Across:** 3 digital 7 conference 8 yawns
9 keyboard 10 photocopier
Down: 1 whistles 2 mugging 4 licence 5 scanner
6 residence

8 1 b 2 b 3 a 4 c 5 b 6 a 7 a 8 a 9 b 10 a

9 1 b 2 c 3 a 4 d 5 a 6 d 7 c 8 b 9 c 10 b

E-mails

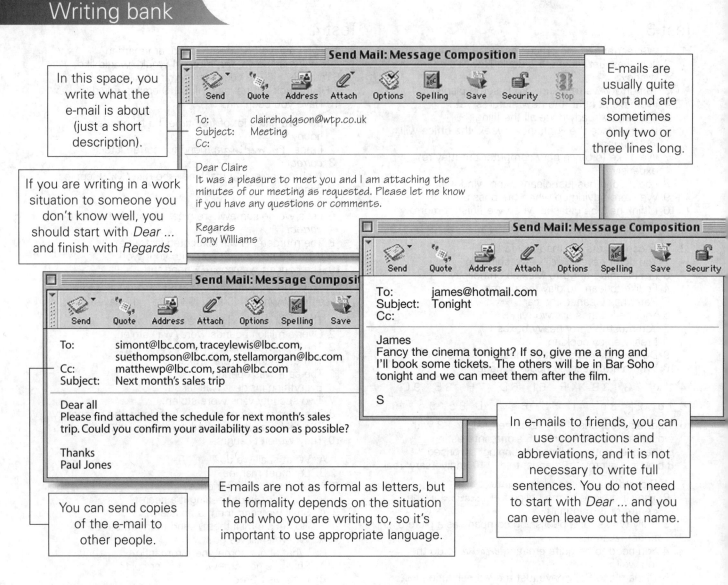

In this space, you write what the e-mail is about (just a short description).

E-mails are usually quite short and are sometimes only two or three lines long.

If you are writing in a work situation to someone you don't know well, you should start with *Dear ...* and finish with *Regards*.

Send Mail: Message Composition

To: clairehodgson@wtp.co.uk
Subject: Meeting
Cc:

Dear Claire
It was a pleasure to meet you and I am attaching the minutes of our meeting as requested. Please let me know if you have any questions or comments.

Regards
Tony Williams

Send Mail: Message Composition

To: james@hotmail.com
Subject: Tonight
Cc:

James
Fancy the cinema tonight? If so, give me a ring and I'll book some tickets. The others will be in Bar Soho tonight and we can meet them after the film.

S

Send Mail: Message Composit

To: simont@lbc.com, traceylewis@lbc.com, suethompson@lbc.com, stellamorgan@lbc.com
Cc: matthewp@lbc.com, sarah@lbc.com
Subject: Next month's sales trip

Dear all
Please find attached the schedule for next month's sales trip. Could you confirm your availability as soon as possible?

Thanks
Paul Jones

In e-mails to friends, you can use contractions and abbreviations, and it is not necessary to write full sentences. You do not need to start with *Dear ...* and you can even leave out the name.

You can send copies of the e-mail to other people.

E-mails are not as formal as letters, but the formality depends on the situation and who you are writing to, so it's important to use appropriate language.

Useful language

- Main message:
  RE: (= regarding)
  I attach ...
  Here is ...
  Let me know if you have any questions.
  Please can you forward this to anyone else who might be interested.
  Please send me your views on the attached document.

- Final sentence:
  Hope to see you soon.
  Please give me a ring.
  See you later.

  Kind regards
  Best regards

Teaching notes

1 Brainstorm who we write e-mails to, and why/when (e.g. friends, family, colleagues/to give news, ask for and send information).

2 Ask students how an e-mail is different from a letter (e.g. shorter, usually less formal, no need to write address or date, often shorter sentences, etc.).

3 Give out the model and go through it with students. For each e-mail, ask what the relationship is between the people and answer any vocabulary questions (the first and last are between work colleagues, the second one is between friends). Then go through the **Useful language** – as you do, ask students the type of situations in which they might use each expression (e.g. with a friend, colleague, boss, etc.).

4 Lesson 3 in the Students' Book gives practice in this type of writing.

Informal letters

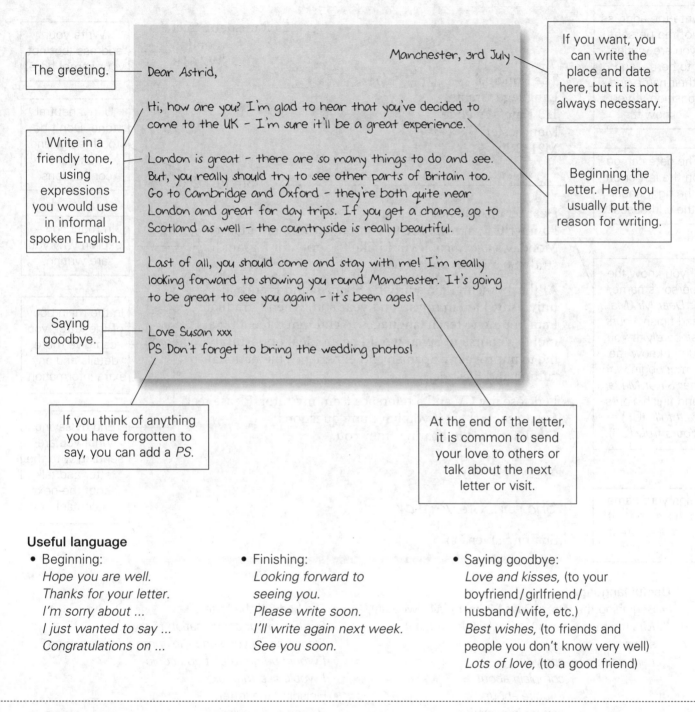

The greeting.

Dear Astrid,

Manchester, 3rd July

If you want, you can write the place and date here, but it is not always necessary.

Write in a friendly tone, using expressions you would use in informal spoken English.

Hi, how are you? I'm glad to hear that you've decided to come to the UK – I'm sure it'll be a great experience.

London is great – there are so many things to do and see. But, you really should try to see other parts of Britain too. Go to Cambridge and Oxford – they're both quite near London and great for day trips. If you get a chance, go to Scotland as well – the countryside is really beautiful.

Last of all, you should come and stay with me! I'm really looking forward to showing you round Manchester. It's going to be great to see you again – it's been ages!

Beginning the letter. Here you usually put the reason for writing.

Saying goodbye.

Love Susan xxx
PS Don't forget to bring the wedding photos!

If you think of anything you have forgotten to say, you can add a *PS*.

At the end of the letter, it is common to send your love to others or talk about the next letter or visit.

Useful language

- Beginning:
  Hope you are well.
  Thanks for your letter.
  I'm sorry about ...
  I just wanted to say ...
  Congratulations on ...

- Finishing:
  Looking forward to seeing you.
  Please write soon.
  I'll write again next week.
  See you soon.

- Saying goodbye:
  Love and kisses, (to your boyfriend / girlfriend / husband / wife, etc.)
  Best wishes, (to friends and people you don't know very well)
  Lots of love, (to a good friend)

Teaching notes

1 Brainstorm who we write informal letters to, and why (e.g. friends, family / to give news, invite, thank, etc.).

2 Ask questions to elicit information about organisation and layout (e.g. Where do we put the date? How do we begin the letter? How do we finish a letter?).

3 Give out the model and go through it with students. Answer any vocabulary questions. Do the same with **Useful language**.

4 Lessons 5, 15 and 28 in the Students' Book give practice in this type of writing.

Formal letters

Write the address of the person you are writing to here – and their name and position, if you know it.

The date can go on the left or on the right under the addresses.

If you know the person's name, put *Dear Mr / Ms ...* and finish *Yours sincerely*. If you don't know the name, begin with *Dear Sir or Madam* and finish *Yours faithfully* (UK) or *Yours truly* (US).

Sign your name and also print it to make sure it is clear.

Write your address (but not your name) here.

Use a neutral tone. Don't be too friendly and don't use contractions.

Introduction – explain why you are writing.

In the main body of the letter, you can give more details and any extra information.

End by saying what you are sending with the letter and talk about the next contact.

---

35 Ramsden Street
London
SW7 6TR

The Principal
Language Grants
113 King's Avenue
Manchester
M21 4RE

13th July 2002

Dear Sir or Madam,
I am writing in response to your advertisement in last Monday's *Guardian*. I would like to apply for a grant to study Spanish in Barcelona.

At the moment, I am studying Spanish and French at university. I am in my second year and, when I graduate, I am hoping to teach languages to children. I feel that a month's course in Spain would be an ideal opportunity for me to improve my Spanish and experience the national culture and lifestyle.

I enclose my CV and a reference from my tutor. Please feel free to contact me if you have any questions.
I look forward to hearing from you.

Yours faithfully,

Sharon Stevenson

Sharon Stevenson

Useful language

- Beginning the letter: *Dear Mr* (man), *Ms* (woman), *Mrs* (married woman), *Miss* (single woman) + surname
  I am writing to apply for ...
  complain about ...
  enquire about ...
  ask for information.

- The body of the letter:
  Further to our conversation today, ...
  Please could you send me some information on ...
  I would be grateful if you could ...
  I would like to book ...
- Finishing the letter:
  Please find enclosed ...
  With thanks in advance,

Teaching notes

1 Brainstorm when we need to write formal letters (e.g. to apply for a job, request information, make a complaint, etc.).

2 Ask questions to elicit information about organisation and layout (e.g. Where do we put the addresses and date? How do we begin the letter? How do we end the letter? etc.).

3 Give out the model, give students time to read the letter and check the answers to Step 2. Go through the **Useful language**, answering any questions about vocabulary.

4 Lesson 8 in the Students' Book gives practice in writing applications.

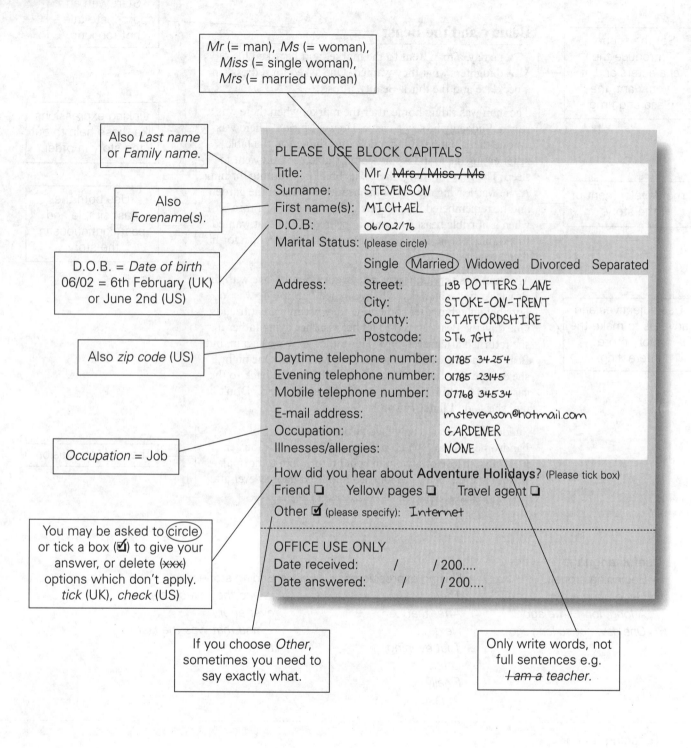

Mr (= man), Ms (= woman), Miss (= single woman), Mrs (= married woman)

Also *Last name* or *Family name.*

Also *Forename(s).*

D.O.B. = *Date of birth* 06/02 = 6th February (UK) or June 2nd (US)

Also *zip code* (US)

Occupation = Job

You may be asked to (circle) or tick a box (☑) to give your answer, or delete (xxx) options which don't apply. *tick* (UK), *check* (US)

If you choose *Other*, sometimes you need to say exactly what.

Only write words, not full sentences e.g. *I am a teacher.*

PLEASE USE BLOCK CAPITALS

Title: Mr / ~~Mrs / Miss / Ms~~
Surname: STEVENSON
First name(s): MICHAEL
D.O.B: 06/02/76
Marital Status: (please circle)

Single (Married) Widowed Divorced Separated

Address:
Street: 13B POTTERS LANE
City: STOKE-ON-TRENT
County: STAFFORDSHIRE
Postcode: ST6 7GH

Daytime telephone number: 01785 34254
Evening telephone number: 01785 23145
Mobile telephone number: 07768 34534
E-mail address: mstevenson@hotmail.com
Occupation: GARDENER
Illnesses/allergies: NONE

How did you hear about **Adventure Holidays**? (Please tick box)
Friend ❑   Yellow pages ❑   Travel agent ❑

Other ☑ (please specify): Internet

OFFICE USE ONLY
Date received: /   / 200....
Date answered: /   / 200....

Teaching notes

1 Brainstorm when we need to fill in forms (e.g. to apply for a job, course, passport, or loan; to join a club).

2 Ask students what information you usually have to give when filling a form (e.g. name, address, marital status, occupation).

3 Give out the model and go through it with students. Answer any vocabulary questions.

4 Lesson 8 in the Students' Book gives practice in this type of writing.

Stories

Beauty and the Beast

Start with an appropriate title – not too long.

Set the scene – introduce the characters and, if you want, the place and time.

O ne day, a man went to the market and he asked his daughters what they wanted. One asked for a dress, one a necklace and the third, Beauty, a rose.

The man was riding home after the market <u>when</u> there was a storm. <u>Suddenly</u> he saw a castle. He went inside. There was no one there, but he found a delicious dinner on the table. <u>After eating</u>, he found a soft, comfortable bed and went to sleep. <u>The next morning</u>, there was breakfast waiting for him. As he was leaving, he saw some beautiful roses in the garden and he remembered his daughter. He <u>was picking</u> a rose, when a horrible beast suddenly <u>appeared</u>. The beast wanted to kill him, but he decided to let the man live in return for his daughter.

The man was <u>very unhappy</u>, but Beauty went to live with the Beast. At first, she was <u>really frightened</u> because he was so <u>horribly ugly</u>, but after some time they became great friends. One day, the Beast agreed to let her visit her dying father if she returned after seven days. Her father grew well again, but Beauty did not realise the seven days were over. One night, she dreamt that the Beast was dying. She rushed back to the castle and found him in the garden, his eyes closed. 'Don't die,' she said, 'I'll marry you.'

Suddenly, the Beast's ugly face turned into the face of a handsome prince! A witch had turned him into a monster, and only the love of a woman could return him to normal. Beauty and the Beast got married and lived happily ever after.

Linking expressions like these help to put the story in order.

The development of the story.

Use both the past simple and past continuous in the story.

Use adjectives and adverbs to make the story more interesting.

The end / conclusion.

Useful language

- Beginning stories:
  Once upon a time ...
  A long, long time ago ...
  One day, not so long ago ...

- Linking expressions:
  Then, ...
  After that, ...
  Next, ...
  That evening, ...
  Later, ...
  Finally, ...
  At last, ...

- Ending stories:
  ... and they lived happily ever after.
  ... and that was the last time ...

Teaching notes

1 Brainstorm some famous stories that have been made into musicals. Ask the students if they know the story of *Beauty and the Beast*.

2 Give out the story, then give students time to read it and ask vocabulary questions.

3 Go through the notes and ask students to underline all the linking expressions. Check the answers, then ask them to underline all the past tenses.

4 Go through the **Useful language** and answer any questions.

5 Lesson 24 in the Students' Book gives practice in this type of writing.

Short notes

You can leave out unnecessary words, such as pronouns and auxiliaries.

Tom
Gone to the shops to get dinner. Will be back before 6 – see you then.
N xxx

John
Please, please don't forget to buy Mum's birthday present today – she's coming to visit TOMORROW!
Mandy

Use capital letters, underlining or exclamation marks for emphasis.

Finish with your name or just your initial.

Use informal language and contractions.

M
Going to the cinema tonight with Mark, so won't be home for dinner. Don't wait up for me!
Susan

Mr Morden rang to say he couldn't come today – can you call him back before 5?
Robert

Use digits instead of spelling out numbers.

Useful language
Remember to ...
Back in 5 minutes.
See you at 10.
Back at 7.
See you later.
Hope you can come tonight.
Ring me before ...
Will ring tomorrow.

Teaching notes

1 Ask students when people need to leave each other notes (e.g. to tell them their plans, ask them to do something, pass on a message, give an explanation, etc.).

2 Elicit what type of language you use in a note (informal, short – only the necessary information).

3 Give out the models and go through them with students. For each one, ask them what the purpose of the note is.

4 Ask students, in pairs, to write a reply for each one. Monitor and correct, and as feedback, ask a few pairs to read out their answers.

5 Lessons 29 and 36 in the Students' Book give practice in this type of writing.

Adverts

Use adjectives, comparatives and superlatives.

It is very common to use imperatives in adverts.

Write in short sentences that attract the attention of the reader.

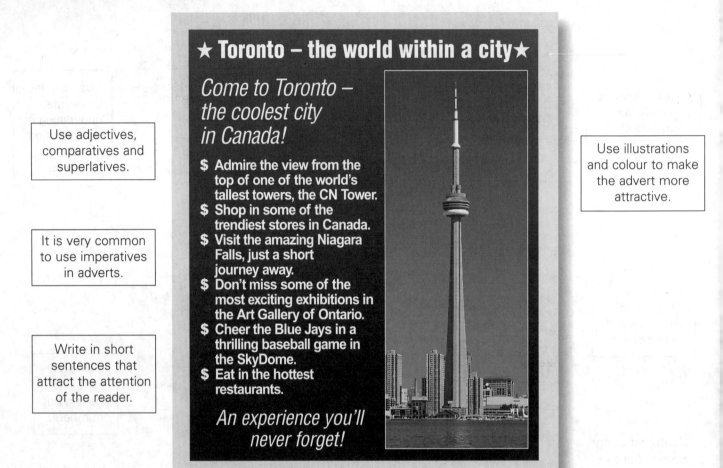

★ **Toronto – the world within a city** ★

Come to Toronto – the coolest city in Canada!

$ **Admire the view from the top of one of the world's tallest towers, the CN Tower.**
$ **Shop in some of the trendiest stores in Canada.**
$ **Visit the amazing Niagara Falls, just a short journey away.**
$ **Don't miss some of the most exciting exhibitions in the Art Gallery of Ontario.**
$ **Cheer the Blue Jays in a thrilling baseball game in the SkyDome.**
$ **Eat in the hottest restaurants.**

An experience you'll never forget!

Use illustrations and colour to make the advert more attractive.

Useful language

- Adjectives:
  incredible
  world-renowned
  trendy
  good value
  satisfying
  amazing
  tasty

- Phrases:
  The best place in town!
  A once-in-a-lifetime experience.
  Don't miss it!
  You have to see it to believe it!
  Don't wait any longer!
  The fastest car on the road.

Teaching notes

1 Brainstorm what type of adverts you can see (e.g. places, products, jobs, etc.). Ask students if they have any favourite adverts.
2 Ask how advertisers attract attention (e.g. photos, colour, short, sharp sentences) and what kind of language they use (adjectives, superlatives, imperatives, exclamations).
3 Give out the model and go through it with students. Answer any vocabulary questions.
4 Lessons 17 and 22 in the Students' Book give practice in this type of writing.